W9-BFY-441

iNterCOM

2000

Jennifer E. Bixby

HH Heinle & Heinle Publishers
A DIVISION OF WADSWORTH, INC.
Boston, Massachusetts 02116

WORKBOOK

Cover: The Graphics Studio/Gerry Rosentswieg

Copyright © 1990
by Heinle & Heinle Publishers under the Universal Copyright
Convention and Pan-American Copyright Convention.

All rights reserved. No part of this publication may be
reproduced or transmitted in any form or by any means, elec-
tronic or mechanical, including photocopy, recording, or any
information storage or retrieval system, without permission in
writing from the publisher. Previously published as *Intercom:
English for International Communication,* Copyright 1977,
and *New Intercom,* Copyright 1984.

Heinle & Heinle Publishers is a division of Wadsworth, Inc.

Manufactured in the United States of America.

ISBN 0-8384-1808-2

10 9 8 7 6 5 4 3 2 1

Contents

Name _____   Date _____

Talking about past events *(text, page 7)*

A How do you pronounce it? Is the past tense ending of each of these verbs pronounced /t/, /d/, or /id/? Add *-ed* or *-d* to each verb, say it to yourself, and then write it in the correct column.

dance, look, study, listen, paint, call, help, stay, want, wash, visit, pass, work, like, play, watch, relax, live, clean, skate

/ t /	/ d /	/ id /
danced	_____	_____
_____	_____	_____
_____	_____	_____
_____	_____	_____
_____	_____	_____
_____	_____	_____
_____	_____	_____
_____	_____	_____
_____	_____	_____

Asking and telling about past events *(text, page 8)*

B Answer the questions. Answer truthfully, using *Yes, I did* or *No, I didn't*. If you answer no, try to say what you *did* do. For numbers 9-12, write and answer your own questions.

1. Did you work yesterday? _____

2. Did you call a friend yesterday? _____

3. Did you cook dinner last night? _____

4. Did you study English last night? _____

5. Did you watch TV last night? _____

6. Did you relax last weekend? _____

7. Did you stay home last Friday night? _____

8. Did you dance last Saturday night? _____

9. Did you _____ ? _____

10. _____ ? _____

11. _____ ? _____

12. _____ ? _____

© Heinle & Heinle Publishers. All rights reserved.

Asking and telling about past events *(text, page 10)*

C **What's the question?** Maria is asking Ann about what she did last Saturday night. Write Maria's questions.

MARIA: _What_ _____?

ANN: I went to a party.

MARIA: Oh really? Was _____?

ANN: Yeah, it was great. There were a lot of people there.

MARIA: Did _____?

ANN: No, I didn't see Tom. But I saw Mark and Al.

MARIA: _____?

ANN: I danced with Mark all night. He's a great dancer!

MARIA: _____?

ANN: They played rock and roll music and some Brazilian music.

MARIA: _____?

ANN: I got home at 11:30.

D **Your weekend.** Think about something interesting you did last weekend. Write answers to these questions. Then write a short paragraph about what you did. Be sure to indent the first line of your paragraph. Give as much information as you can.

1. Where did you go last weekend? _____

2. When did you go there? _____

3. Did you go with a friend or a family member? _____

4. Did you go by car or by bus? Did you walk? _____

5. What did you do there? _____

6. Was it fun? interesting? boring? exciting? _____

7. What time did you get home? _____

_____

_____

_____

_____

_____

_____

_____

_____

Name _____ Date _____

Movies *(text, page 11)*

E Crossword puzzle. Complete the puzzle.

Across

4. "Indiana Jones" movies are usually very ____ . There's always a lot of action.
7. The movie was a love story, so it was very ____ .
11. A ____ is a movie that tells an interesting story.
12. Joyce likes interesting and exciting movies. She likes ____ movies.
13. My friend and I cried during the movie. It was very ____ .
14. In a ____ , you are sure to see cowboys, horses, and guns.
15. Something silly is usually ____ . It makes you laugh.

Down

1. Before you go into a movie, you have to buy a ____ .
2. "Dracula" is a very ____ movie.
3. "Dracula" is a ____ movie.
5. The opposite of boring is ____ .
6. If you like a movie you say, "It's a ____ movie."
8. Ted likes ____ because they are funny.
9. The place that shows a movie is called a movie ____ .
10. If you don't like a movie, you can say it's stupid or ____ .

F **What did you think?** Did you see a movie last week or last month? What did you see? What kind of movie was it? Did you enjoy it? Why? Write a few sentences about the movie.

_____

_____

_____

_____

© Heinle & Heinle Publishers. All rights reserved.

Talking about past events *(text, page 12)*

G Interview.   Using the words given, write ten questions to ask your partner. Start each question with *Did you*. Write your own questions for 11 and 12. Then ask your partner the questions and circle *yes* or *no*.

Example			
go / school / yesterday	*Did you go to school yesterday?*	yes	(no)

1. watch TV / last night _____ yes   no
2. study English / last night _____ yes   no
3. have coffee / this morning _____ yes   no
4. go shopping / last weekend _____ yes   no
5. see / *(name of a movie)* _____ yes   no
6. go to a party / last weekend _____ yes   no
7. get home late / Friday night _____ yes   no
8. make dinner / last night _____ yes   no
9. stay home / Saturday night _____ yes   no
10. go to bed early / last night _____ yes   no
11. _____ yes   no
12. _____ yes   no

Now write about your partner. Use the information above to write sentences from each answer. You can add any additional information.

Example
Minh didn't go to school yesterday because she was sick.

1. _____
2. _____
3. _____
4. _____
5. _____
6. _____
7. _____
8. _____
9. _____
10. _____
11. _____
12. _____

Making suggestions; refusing and accepting *(text, page 14)*

H **Free time activities.** What do you like to do with your friends in your free time? Write short conversations. Make a suggestion. Your friend accepts or refuses.

> **Example**
>
> A: *Why don't we go to the movies tonight?*
> B: *Sorry, I can't. I have to study for a test.*

1. A: _____

   B: _____

2. A: _____

   B: _____

3. A: _____

   B: _____

I **Making plans.** Look at Susan's schedule for this week. In the next column, fill in your own schedule. In the conversation below, call Susan and make a suggestion to do something. Complete the conversation. Use as many lines as you need.

Time	Susan	You
Tonight	computer class	
Thursday	free after 9 PM	
Friday	free	
Saturday	Julio's birthday party	

SUSAN: Hello.

YOU: Hi, Susan. It's _____ . How _____ ?

SUSAN: I'm fine, _____ . How about you?

YOU: _____ . I'm calling because I'm free _____ .

Why don't we _____ ?

SUSAN: _____

YOU: _____

SUSAN: _____

YOU: _____

SUSAN: _____

YOU: _____

© Heinle & Heinle Publishers. All rights reserved.

J **How was your day?** Think about your day yesterday. Look at these questions and then write a paragraph about your day. Include as much information as you can.

Questions: How was your day yesterday? Were you busy? What time did you get up? What did you have for breakfast? Where did you go? What did you do in the morning? in the afternoon? When did you get home? What did you do at home? Did you make dinner? Did you go to bed early or late?

_____

_____

_____

_____

_____

_____

_____

_____

_____

K **Talk about it.** Exchange papers with a partner. Read your partner's paragraph. Ask your partner to explain anything you don't understand. Can you help make the paragraph better? Ask questions about your partner's day and make suggestions for the paragraph. Then have your partner do the same with your paragraph.

Now rewrite your paragraph, making corrections and improvements. Is your paragraph better than before?

_____

_____

_____

_____

_____

_____

_____

_____

_____

Name _____ Date _____

Unit 2	**Is There a Bank Near Here?**

Describing location *(text, page 18)*

A Where's the bank? In the space below, draw a map of your city or town. Include street names and as many places as you can. Then write sentences about locations on the map. Use *at the corner of, between,* and *at the end of.*

Example

First State Bank is at the corner of Main Street and South Street.

1. _____

2. _____

3. _____

4. _____

5. _____

6. _____

7. _____

8. _____

9. _____

10. _____

© Heinle & Heinle Publishers. All rights reserved.

Talking about location with *there is (there's)* (text, page 19)

B **Street locations.** Give information about places in your city or town. You can use your map from exercise A.

> **Example**
> *There's a bank on Main Street.*

1. _____
2. _____
3. _____
4. _____
5. _____
6. _____
7. _____
8. _____

Asking about location with *there is:* questions and short affirmative answers *(text, page 20)*

C **Places in your town or city.** Your friend is new to your city or town. He or she is asking you questions about where things are. Write short conversations.

> **Example**
> A: *Is there a park in Boston?*
> B: *Yes, there is.*
> A: *Where is it?*
> B: *It's on Arlington Street.*

1. A: _____
   B: _____
   A: _____
   B: _____
2. A: _____
   B: _____
   A: _____
   B: _____
3. A: _____
   B: _____
   A: _____
   B: _____

4. A: _____
   B: _____
   A: _____
   B: _____
5. A: _____
   B: _____
   A: _____
   B: _____
6. A: _____
   B: _____
   A: _____
   B: _____

Name _____   Date _____

Map directions *(text, page 21)*

D **Follow directions.** Read the directions and draw the places on the map of Southboro. The first one is done for you.

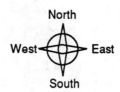

1. Draw a park in the middle of the map.

2. Draw an airport south of the park.

3. Draw a train station east of the airport.

4. Draw a lake west of the airport.

5. Draw a big factory north of the lake and west of the park.

6. Draw a mall north of the factory.

7. Draw a supermarket east of the mall and north of the park.

8. Draw houses east of the park and north of the train station.

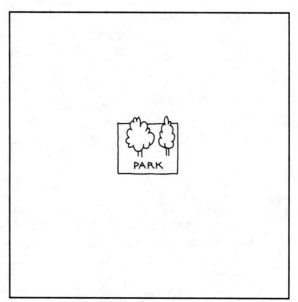

E **Describe the city.** Write a paragraph about the city of Southboro. Tell what is in the city and where places are. Write with a pencil and be sure to indent the first line of your paragraph.

_____

_____

_____

_____

_____

_____

_____

_____

_____

_____

Now ask your partner to read your paragraph and suggest changes. Do you agree with the changes he or she suggests?

© Heinle & Heinle Publishers. All rights reserved.

Asking about location with *there is:* short negative answers *(text, page 22)*

F   **What's in your city or town?** Look at the list of places and buildings. Do you have
these in your city or town? Check *yes* or *no*.

yes	no		yes	no	
____	____	bus station	____	____	train station
____	____	city hall	____	____	hotel
____	____	park	____	____	zoo
____	____	art museum	____	____	lake
____	____	science museum	____	____	river
____	____	mall	____	____	college or university
____	____	airport	____	____	subway
____	____	factory	____	____	TV studio
____	____	beach			

G   **Is there a . . . ?** There is a new student from China in your class. Her name is Mei Lin.
She's asking you about your city or town. Using the information from exercise E,
write short conversations.

> **Examples**
>
> MEI LIN: *Is there an airport?*   MEI LIN: *Is there a train station?*
> YOU: *Yes, there is. It's south of*   YOU: *No, there isn't, but there's*
>   *the bus station.*   *a bus station.*

1. MEI LIN: _____

   YOU: _____

2. MEI LIN: _____

   YOU: _____

3. MEI LIN: _____

   YOU: _____

4. MEI LIN: _____

   YOU: _____

5. MEI LIN: _____

   YOU: _____

6. MEI LIN: _____

   YOU: _____

Name _____ Date _____

Asking for and giving directions *(text, page 24)*

H **Give directions.** The new student in your class, Mei Lin, needs directions from your school to different places in your town or city. Write the name of the place, and then write directions. You can use these expressions: *go north / south / east / west; take the first / second / third street on your right / left; turn; walk.*

1. Directions to _____

_____

_____

_____

_____

2. Directions to _____

_____

_____

_____

_____

3. Directions to _____

_____

_____

_____

_____

4. Directions to _____

_____

_____

_____

_____

© Heinle & Heinle Publishers. All rights reserved.

I **Map completion.** Read the statements below. Fill in the missing labels on the map.

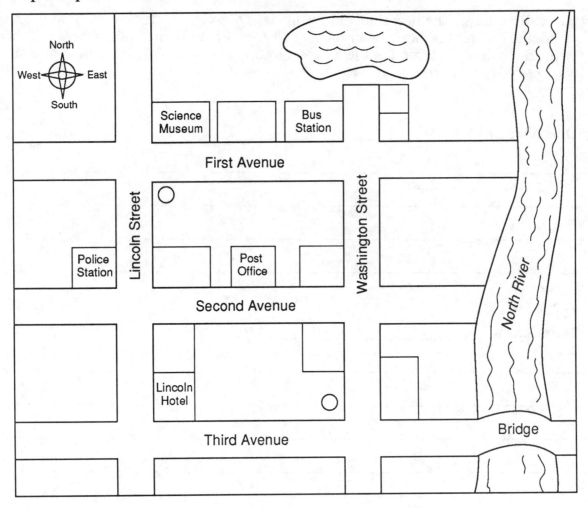

1. City Hall is at the corner of Lincoln Street and Second Avenue, across from the police station.

2. The post office is between City Hall and Hill's Department Store.

3. First National Bank is at the corner of Lincoln Street and Second Avenue, across from City Hall and next to the Lincoln Hotel.

4. The library is on First Avenue, between the Science Museum and the bus station.

5. Dino's Italian Restaurant is at the end of First Avenue.

6. Mann's Coffee Shop is on Washington Street, next to Dino's Italian Restaurant.

7. Lake George is at the end of Washington Street.

8. The Washington Hotel is at the corner of Washington Street and Third Avenue, next to the bridge.

9. There are two subway stations. One is at the corner of Washington Street and Third Avenue, across from the Washington Hotel. The other is on the corner of Lincoln Street and First Avenue, across from the Science Museum.

10. Smith's Office Building is at the corner of Second Avenue and Washington Street, across from Hill's Department Store.

Name _____ Date _____

J **Role play.** Work with a partner. First, compare your maps from page 12. Do you both have the same information in the same places? Check your work together. Then pick a starting place. Give directions to another place on your map, but don't tell your partner the place. Your partner follows your directions. Can your partner get to the place and not get lost? Take turns giving directions to several places on the map.

> **Example**
>
> A: _Start at the First National Bank. Go north on Lincoln Street and take your second right. That's First Avenue. Walk one block. It's on the corner of Washington Street and First Avenue, next to the library._
> B: _Is it the bus station?_
> A: _That's right._

K **Write it down!** Write down directions from one place to another on the map.

1. _____
_____
_____
_____
_____

2. _____
_____
_____
_____
_____

3. _____
_____
_____
_____
_____

© Heinle & Heinle Publishers. All rights reserved.

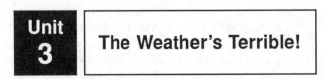

Unit 3 The Weather's Terrible!

Describing the weather *(text, page 28)*

A **Weather map.** Look at the weather map of the United States. Write about the weather in each of the cities.

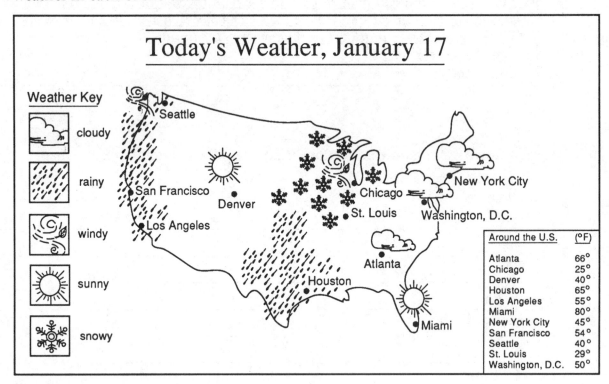

Today's Weather, January 17

Weather Key
- cloudy
- rainy
- windy
- sunny
- snowy

Around the U.S.	(°F)
Atlanta	66°
Chicago	25°
Denver	40°
Houston	65°
Los Angeles	55°
Miami	80°
New York City	45°
San Francisco	54°
Seattle	40°
St. Louis	29°
Washington, D.C.	50°

What's the weather like in . . . ?

> **Example**
>
> (Seattle) *In Seattle it's cool, rainy, and windy today.*

1. (Atlanta) _____

2. (Chicago) _____

3. (Denver) _____

4. (Houston) _____

5. (Los Angeles) _____

6. (Miami) _____

7. (New York) _____

8. (San Francisco) _____

9. (St. Louis) _____

10. (Washington, D.C.) _____

Name _____   Date _____

Contrasting: simple present versus present continuous *(text, page 29)*

B **Weather questions.** Read the notes about typical January weather in some U.S. cities. Imagine that today is January 17. Look at the map of "today's weather" on page 14 to answer the questions.

> *typical January weather* - _snow_ in Chicago, Denver, New York City, and St. Louis
> _rain_ in Atlanta, San Francisco, and Seattle

Example	
Does it rain a lot in Chicago in January?	*No, it doesn't.*
Is it raining in Chicago now?	*No, it isn't. It's snowing.*

1. Is it raining in Seattle now? _____
2. Is it snowing in Chicago now? _____
3. Is it snowing in New York City now? _____
4. Does it snow in New York in January? _____
5. Is it raining in Miami now? _____
6. Does it rain a lot in Denver in January? _____
7. Is it raining in San Francisco now? _____
8. Does it rain a lot in San Francisco in January? _____
9. Does it snow a lot in Atlanta in January? _____
10. Is it raining in Atlanta now? _____

C **Compare the weather.** Compare typical January weather with weather "today's weather" shown on the map on page 14. Write statements with *and* or *but*.

Example	
(Seattle) *It rains a lot in Seattle in January, and it's raining there today.*	

1. (Atlanta) _____

_____

2. (Chicago) _____

_____

3. (New York City) _____

_____

4. (San Francisco) _____

_____

5. (St. Louis) _____

_____

6. (Denver) _____

_____

© Heinle & Heinle Publishers. All rights reserved.

Asking for and giving temperatures *(text, page 30)*

D **Weather around the world.** Using information from the chart, answer the questions.

Cities around the world				
City	Today's Weather	Temp. (°F)	Yesterday's Weather	Temp. (°F)
Caracas	sunny	64°	cloudy	60°
São Paulo	sunny	66°	sunny	70°
Berlin	cloudy	52°	rainy	40°
Cairo	rainy	63°	rainy	60°
Hong Kong	cloudy	68°	rainy	63°
London	rainy	45°	cloudy	54°
Moscow	snowy	17°	snowy	19°
Rome	sunny	50°	sunny	55°
San José	rainy	61°	cloudy	59°
Tokyo	cloudy	43°	sunny	45°

Example

What's the weather in Tokyo today?   *It's cloudy and 43°.*

1. What's the weather in Moscow today? _____

2. What was the weather in Caracas yesterday? _____

3. What's the weather in London today? _____

4. What was the weather in San José yesterday? _____

5. What's the weather in Hong Kong today? _____

6. What's the weather in São Paulo today? _____

7. What was the weather in Berlin yesterday? _____

8. What's the weather in Cairo today? _____

9. What was the weather in Tokyo yesterday? _____

10. What was the weather in Rome yesterday? _____

E **Weather report.** Write weather reports about two cities, using information from the chart.

Example

Today the temperature in London is 45°. It's rainy and cool. Yesterday London was cool and cloudy. The temperature was 54°.

1. _____

_____

2. _____

_____

Talking about the past   *(text, page 32-33)*
Explaining past actions   *(text, page 33)*

F   **Fill in the blank.** Read Sandro's story about his ski trip. Complete the paragraph with the correct past tense form of the verb in parenthesis.

Saturday morning the weather *was* (be) great for skiing! It _____ (snow) Friday night, and when I _____ (get) up Saturday morning, there were six inches of snow on the ground! I _____ (call) my friend Marta and _____ (invite) her to go skiing. We _____ (get) to the ski area at 8:30. It _____ (be) cloudy and cool. It _____ (be) about 40°. The snow was beautiful. We _____ (have) a great time and we skied for three hours. At 1:00 we _____ (eat) lunch. But after lunch, it _____ (start) to rain! The skiing _____ (be) terrible. So, we _____ (go) to the car, but the car didn't start. There was no gas in the car. We _____ (walk) to the gas station and _____ (get) more gas. We finally _____ (get) home at 7:00, tired, wet, and hungry. What a day!

G   **Answer the questions.** Write the answers to the questions about Sandro's ski trip.

1. Did it snow on Friday? _____

2. When did Sandro and his friend go skiing? _____

3. What time did they get to the ski area? _____

4. How long did they ski? _____

5. Did they ski all day? _____

6. Why didn't they ski after lunch? _____

7. Did the car start? _____

8. Why didn't the car start? _____

9. Did they drive to the gas station? _____

10. What time did they get home? _____

H   **True or false?** Read each statement about Sandro's ski trip. Circle True or False.

True	False	1. The weather was terrible Saturday morning.
True	False	2. It snowed Friday night.
True	False	3. Sandro invited two friends to go skiing.
True	False	4. They got to the ski area at 10:30.
True	False	5. It was about 40° at the ski area.
True	False	6. They had a good time skiing before lunch.
True	False	7. It rained after lunch.
True	False	8. They went home early because they were tired of skiing.
True	False	9. They skied to the gas station for gas.
True	False	10. They got home at 7:00 PM.

© Heinle & Heinle Publishers. All rights reserved.

I The four seasons. Think about the four seasons in your town or city, or where you are from. Fill in the chart with notes about typical weather. You may want to use some of the adjectives listed to describe the weather.

Vocabulary: great / terrible / awful / wonderful / OK / rainy / snowy / cloudy / windy / sunny / dry (no rain) / cold / cool / warm / hot

Example

Place: _Boston_

Season	Weather	Temperature	Favorite activities
spring	_cool, sometimes sunny sometimes rainy_	_50-60 degrees_	_ride a bike, walk, go on a picnic_

Place: _____

Season	Weather	Temperature	Favorite activities
spring			
summer			
winter			
fall			

J Writing from notes. Use your notes from exercise I to write two paragraphs about two seasons in your city or town, or where you are from. Remember to indent the first line of your paragraphs. When you are finished, ask your partner to check your writing for punctuation and spelling.

Example

     In Boston, the spring is nice. It's sometimes rainy and sometimes sunny. The days are cool. The temperature is from 50 to 60 degrees. In the spring, I like to ride a bike, walk, or go on a picnic.

_____

_____

_____

_____

_____

_____

_____

Name _____   Date _____

Pointing out things far from you *(text, page 38)*

A **Conversation completion.** Fill in the blanks to complete the conversations. Use *that, those,* or *one.*

1. FRED: Do you like _____ T-shirt, Tim?
   TIM: No, but I like the blue _____ , next to the red shirt.
   FRED: Hey! How about the red _____ for me?
   TIM: Sure. _____ color looks good on you.

2. SANDRA: May I try on _____ shorts?
   SALESPERSON: Certainly. These?
   SANDRA: No, _____ blue shorts, next to the black ones.

3. ANA: Do you like _____ dress?
   MARIA: Which _____ ?
   ANA: The black and white _____ , next to the purple _____ .
   MARIA: Sure. _____ dress is beautiful! Try it on.

4. BOB: Alan, let's look over there in that window. I need some new shoes.
   ALAN: Try _____ shoes on. They aren't expensive.
   BOB: I don't know. I don't like the color. How about _____ shoes, next to the boots.
   ALAN: _____ shoes are fine, too. Let's go inside and ask for some help.

Clothes *(text, page 40)*

B **Scrambled words.** Each clothing word is scrambled. Write the word in the blank.

> **Example**
>
> ite *tie*

1. cetkaj	*j*_____	10. tah _____
2. rasfc	*s*_____	11. legvos _____
3. sotob	*b*_____	12. raswete _____
4. stapn	_____	13. tcao _____
5. kesnaers	_____	14. risth _____
6. salsdan	_____	15. kistr _____
7. sanej	_____	16. resds _____
8. ohses	_____	17. tosrhs _____
9. itsu	_____	18. solube _____

© Heinle & Heinle Publishers. All rights reserved.

C **What are you wearing?** Write about what you are wearing now. Then write about three other people (classmates, friends, family members). Be sure to tell what color each thing is.

> **Example**
>
> *I am wearing a white sweater, a red shirt, and black pants. I'm wearing black and gray socks and brown shoes.*

1. _____

_____

2. _____

_____

3. _____

_____

4. _____

_____

D **Going on a trip.** Read about each imaginary trip below. Then write a list of what clothes you need. Then compare your lists with your classmates'.

1. You are going to the beach for five days. You are going for a vacation. It is very hot and sunny there.

I need _____

_____

_____

2. You are going to New York City. It's December and it's very cold in New York. You are going to stay for three days. There is a party on one of the nights.

I need _____

_____

_____

3. You are going to visit a friend in Chicago in May. You are going to be there for five days. The weather there is warm during the day and cool at night. Sometimes it can be hot in May.

I need _____

_____

_____

Name _____ Date _____

Explaining problems with clothes *(text, page 42)*

E How does it fit? Write a conversation for each picture.

Example	

 SALESPERSON: *How does it fit?*
CUSTOMER: *I think it's too long.*

1.   SALESPERSON: _____

    CUSTOMER: _____

2.  SALESPERSON: _____

    CUSTOMER: _____

3.   SALESPERSON: _____

    CUSTOMER: _____

4.   SALESPERSON: _____

    CUSTOMER: _____

5.   SALESPERSON: _____

    CUSTOMER: _____

6.   SALESPERSON: _____

    CUSTOMER: _____

7.  SALESPERSON: _____

    CUSTOMER: _____

8.  SALESPERSON: _____

    CUSTOMER: _____

© Heinle & Heinle Publishers. All rights reserved.

Identifying an alternative *(text, page 43)*
Asking for an alternative in a store *(text, page 44)*

F **A difficult customer.** In each situation, the customer asks to see a different color. Write out each conversation. Choose a different color.

> **Example**
>
> The customer is looking at a red scarf.
>
> SALESPERSON: *How do you like the scarf?*
> CUSTOMER: *It's fine, but I'd like a purple one instead.*
> SALESPERSON: *I'm sorry, but we don't have a purple one.*

1. The customer is looking at a blue car.

   SALESPERSON: _____

   CUSTOMER: _____

   SALESPERSON: _____

2. The customer is looking at an orange sweater.

   SALESPERSON: _____

   CUSTOMER: _____

   SALESPERSON: _____

3. The customer is looking at a brown chair.

   SALESPERSON: _____

   CUSTOMER: _____

   SALESPERSON: _____

4. The customer is looking at a black piano.

   SALESPERSON: _____

   CUSTOMER: _____

   SALESPERSON: _____

5. The customer is looking at a blue and white suit.

   SALESPERSON: _____

   CUSTOMER: _____

   SALESPERSON: _____

Name _____   Date _____

Asking for information in a store *(text, page 45)*

G In a department store. You are on the first floor of Foley's Department Store. Ask a salesperson where things are.

DIRECTORY

First Floor: Women's clothes, Women's shoes, Men's and Women's hats and gloves, Jewelry
Second Floor: Women's suits and coats, Men's suits and coats, Men's shoes
Third Floor: Children's clothes, Children's shoes, Sports equipment
Fourth Floor: Dishes, Kitchen supplies, Radios, Tape players, Televisons

---

Example

(women's suits)

A: *Excuse me. Are the women's suits on this floor?*
B: *No, they aren't. They're on the second floor.*

1. (men's sneakers)

   A: _____

   B: _____

2. (boys' jeans)

   A: _____

   B: _____

3. (women's sweaters)

   A: _____

   B: _____

4. (tennis rackets)

   A: _____

   B: _____

5. (men's coats)

   A: _____

   B: _____

6. (men's gloves)

   A: _____

   B: _____

7. (dishes)

   A: _____

   B: _____

8. (women's boots)

   A: _____

   B: _____

© Heinle & Heinle Publishers. All rights reserved.

Final Activities

H **Role play.** Role play the following situation with a partner. Take turns being the salesperson and the customer. The customer asks the salesperson for a coat or jacket. Use your own ideas, colors, etc. Perform the role play at least twice.

SALESPERSON: _____ help you?

CUSTOMER: Yes. May I see that _____ ?

SALESPERSON: _____ course. Which _____ , _____ ?

CUSTOMER: The _____ one, next to _____ .

(The customer tries it on.)

SALESPERSON: How does the _____ fit?

CUSTOMER: Fine, but I don't like the color. May I see

_____ , please?

OR Yes, but it's too _____ . Do you have

_____ ?

SALESPERSON: Of course.

OR I'm _____ . I don't have _____ .

I **Your turn.** You go to a store to buy some clothes. Write a conversation between yourself and a salesperson. Begin the conversation by asking for information about where something is in the store. You can write this with a partner and role play it for the class.

A: _____

B: _____

A: _____

B: _____

A: _____

B: _____

A: _____

B: _____

A: _____

B: _____

Name _____ Date _____

Natural materials *(text, page 49)*
Asking about materials *(text, pages 49-50)*

A **What's it made of?** Ask and answer questions about the pictures.

Example

A: What's *this shirt made of?*
B: *It's made of cotton.*

1. A: What's _____ ?

   B: _____

2. A: Are these _____ cotton ?

   B: _____

3. A: What's _____ ?

   B: _____

4. A: Is _____ ?

   B: _____

5. A: What _____ ?

   B: _____

6. A: Is _____ wool ?

   B: _____

7. A: What _____ ?

   B: _____

8. A: What _____ ?

   B: _____

9. A: Are _____ ?

   B: _____

10. A: _____ ?

    B: _____

© Heinle & Heinle Publishers. All rights reserved.

Metals and jewelry *(text, page 50)*
Giving detailed descriptions *(text, page 51)*

B On sale! Look at the advertisement. Each person wants to buy something at the sale. Write a sentence about each person, giving detailed information.

Mid–winter Sale! Thursday through Saturday!	
Wool and silk scarves - 30% off	ALL Jewelry - 35% off
Leather gloves - 30% off	Copper bracelets and necklaces
Leather jackets - 20% off	Gold and silver necklaces, earrings, and rings
Wool coats - 30% off	
Silk blouses - 20% off	
Cotton and wool sweaters - 40% off	

Example

Mario wants to buy a scarf. *He's going to look at wool and silk scarves.*

1. Van wants to buy a jacket. *He's* _____
2. Alicia wants to buy a blouse. _____
3. Mike wants to buy some gloves. _____
4. Mrs. Chang wants to buy a ring. _____
5. Pete wants to buy a sweater. _____
6. Olga wants to buy a pair of earrings. _____
7. Luisa wants to buy a bracelet. _____
8. Kim wants to buy a coat. _____
9. Sally wants to buy a necklace. _____
10. Ana wants to buy some copper jewelry. _____

Talking about purchases *(text, page 52)*

C What did they buy? Use your imagination to think about what people bought at the sale in exercise B. Write questions and answers about five people from exercise B.

Example

What did Mario buy?   *He bought a wool scarf.*

1. _____   _____
2. _____   _____
3. _____   _____
4. _____   _____
5. _____   _____

Name _____ Date _____

D **What did you buy?** Answer questions about purchases you made. Give details when you can.

> **Example**
>
> Did you go to the supermarket? *Yes, I went last Friday.* OR *No, I didn't.*
> What did you buy? *I bought some bread, some bananas, and some milk.*

1. Did you go to the supermarket? _____

   What did you buy? _____

2. Did you go to the drugstore? _____

   What did you buy? _____

3. Did you go to a department store? _____

   What did you buy? _____

4. Did you go to a bookstore? _____

   What did you buy? _____

Asking for and giving information about where things are made *(text, page 53)*

E **Was it made in . . . ?** Write questions and answers, following the example.

> **Example**
>
> calculator / Korea // Japan
> *Was that calculator made in Korea?*   *No, it was made in Japan.*

1. leather jacket / Italy // Argentina

   _____   _____

2. wool sweater / U.S. // Ireland

   _____   _____

3. leather shoes / Spain // U.S.

   _____   _____

4. chocolate / France // Switzerland

   _____   _____

5. TV / Taiwan // Korea

   _____   _____

6. copper bracelet / Mexico // Colombia

   _____   _____

7. silver necklace / U.S. // Canada

   _____   _____

8. gold ring / Colombia // Peru

   _____   _____

© Heinle & Heinle Publishers. All rights reserved.

Talking about imports and exports *(text, page 53)*

F **Imports and exports.** Look at the illustration. Write statements about imports and exports.

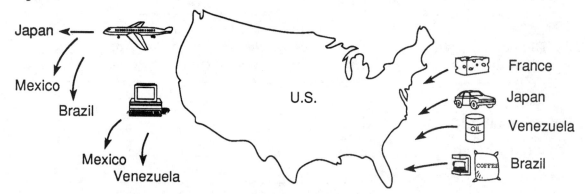

Example
The United States imports oil from Venezuela.
Brazil exports coffee to the United States.

1. _____
2. _____
3. _____
4. _____
5. _____
6. _____
7. _____
8. _____
9. _____
10. _____

G **What's the question?** Using the information in exercise F, write questions about what the U.S. *imports from* and *exports to* different countries.

Example	
What does the U.S. import from France?	It imports cheese.

1. _____ It imports coffee.

2. _____ It exports airplanes.

3. _____ It imports oil.

4. _____ It exports computers.

5. _____ It imports cars.

Name _____   Date _____

Crops *(text, page 55)*
Talking about a country's crops *(text, page 56)*

H   Crops in the United States. The table below shows crops grown by some states in the United States. Write questions and answers about the information.

State	Wheat	Corn	Cotton	Potatoes
Alabama	•	•	•	•
Colorado	•	•		•
Florida	•	•	•	•
Indiana	•	•		•
Maine				•
Massachusetts				•
New Mexico	•	•	•	•
Washington	•	•		•

Example	
What does Alabama grow?	*It grows wheat, corn, cotton, and potatoes.*

1. _____   _____
2. _____   _____
3. _____   _____
4. _____   _____
5. _____   _____
6. _____   _____
7. _____   _____

I   Write about your state. If possible, do this exercise with a partner or in a small group. Think about the state or area you are living in now. What crops does it grow? Write sentences about what crops your state or area grows.

_____

_____

_____

_____

© Heinle & Heinle Publishers. All rights reserved.

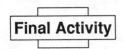

J **Crossword puzzle.** Complete the puzzle.

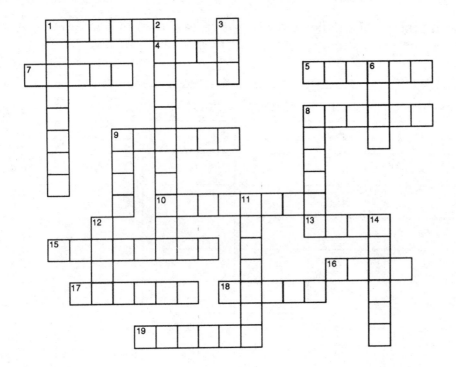

Across
1. The opposite of import
4. A popular food in China, Japan, Thailand, and Vietnam
5. Past tense of *buy*
7. Wheat, sugarcane, and beans are ____ .
8. A strong, dark, hot drink; many South American countries export it.
9. A material used to make shirts, blouses, dresses, and pants
10. Jewelry worn around the neck
13. You wear this jewelry on a finger.
15. Jewelry worn on the wrist
16. A material from sheep, used for warm clothes
17. Copper and silver are ____ .
18. This is used to make bread, cereal, and spaghetti.
19. Mexico is famous for its copper and ____ jewelry.

Down
1. Jewelry worn on the ears
2. Apple pie, brownies, and ice cream are ____ American desserts.
3. A popular hot drink in Japan and England
6. You often give someone a *g*___ on his or her birthday.
8. This metal is used in jewelry. The chemical symbol is Cu.
9. This crop grows in many parts of the United States. It is a yellow vegetable.
11. This natural material is used for shoes, gloves, and jackets.
12. This blouse is ____ of silk.
14. You wear these on your hands to keep them warm.

Name _____ Date _____

A Wonderful Trip!

Unit 6

Numbers from 120 to 99,000 *(text, page 60)*

A **Write it out.** Read the numbers and write them out in words.

Example
46,375 *forty-six thousand three hundred seventy-five*

1. 299 _____

2. 18,000 _____

3. 1,201 _____

4. 9,646 _____

5. 308 _____

6. 50,788 _____

7. 505 _____

8. 1,300 _____

9. 4,367 _____

10. 99,999 _____

Places to visit *(text, page 61)*
Describing places with *there are* *(text, page 62)*

B **Places to visit.** Think about places you visited and places you would like to visit. Look at the list below and check places you visited or want to visit. Write down where the place is. For #8, fill in a place. If you're in class, share your list with a partner. Ask your partner questions about the places he or she visited.

Place	Visited	Want to visit	Where?
Example			
beach	✓	___	*in Miami*

1. beach   ___   ___   _____

2. mountain   ___   ___   _____

3. temple   ___   ___   _____

4. historic building ___   ___   _____

5. park   ___   ___   _____

6. museum   ___   ___   _____

7. lake or river   ___   ___   _____

8. _____   ___   ___   _____

© Heinle & Heinle Publishers. All rights reserved.

C **Write about it.** Use the information you gave in exercise B on page 31. Write sentences about places you visited or would like to visit. Use some of the vocabulary listed to describe the places.

Vocabulary: beautiful / interesting / wonderful / great / exciting / high / fantastic

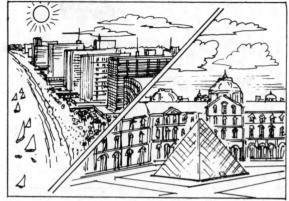

Example
I went to Miami because there are beautiful beaches in Miami. *I'd like to go to Paris because there are wonderful museums in Paris.*

1. _____

2. _____

3. _____

4. _____

5. _____

6. _____

7. _____

8. _____

Yes/no questions with *there are;* short answers *(text, page 63)*

D **Questions about the room.** Where are you right now? Look at the room around you. Using the words given, write questions and answers about the room.

Example		
(chairs)	*Are there any chairs?*	*Yes, there are. There are three chairs.*

1. (chairs) _____ _____

2. (windows) _____ _____

3. (books) _____ _____

4. (people) _____ _____

5. (closets) _____ _____

6. (beds) _____ _____

7. (telephones) _____ _____

8. (teachers) _____ _____

Name _____   Date _____

Possessive adjective *its* (text, page 63)

E **Matching.** Do you know about these cities in the U.S.? Try to match each
city with what it is famous for. Write the number next to the correct letter.
(Hint: Do the cities you know first; then guess on the others.)

City   **Is Famous For**

1. Miami, Florida   ___ a. jazz music and good food
2. Seattle, Washington   ___ b. movie stars and warm weather
3. New York City, New York   ___ c. beautiful beaches, mountains, and flowers
4. Los Angeles, California   ___ d. the Empire State Building, the United Nations
5. New Orleans, Louisiana   ___ e. government buildings and the White House
6. Santa Fe, New Mexico   _1_ f. beautiful beaches and hotels
7. Washington, D.C.   ___ g. rain, fog, seafood, and views of Mt. Rainier
8. Honolulu, Hawaii   ___ h. museums, parks, modern buildings, and windy
9. San Francisco, California   weather
10. Chicago, Illinois   ___ i. Indian art and culture, Mexican food, and skiing
                               ___ j. hills, cable cars, and the Golden Gate Bridge

F **What's it famous for?** Write a sentence about each of the cities in exercise E.

> **Example**
>
> *Miami is famous for its beautiful beaches and hotels.*

1. _____
2. _____
3. _____
4. _____
5. _____
6. _____
7. _____
8. _____
9. _____

G **Your turn!** What is your native country (or the town or city you are living in) famous
for? Write a short paragraph. Indent the first line of your paragraph.

> **Example**
>
> *I am Colombian. Colombia is famous for its beautiful beaches and*
> *countryside. There are many mountains and rivers. There are many historical*
> *ruins, too. It is famous for its coffee, gold, emeralds, and copper.*

_____

_____

_____

_____

© Heinle & Heinle Publishers. All rights reserved.

Describing places *(text, page 65)*
Asking for and giving information about length, depth, width, and height
(text, pages 66-67)

H   Map work.   Read the statements below and label the places on the map.

1. One of the major rivers in the U.S. is the **Mississippi River**. It begins
   in the northern central state of Minnesota and flows down through
   many midwestern states. It goes through St. Louis, and continues
   through the south. It ends in Louisiana, near New Orleans, and flows
   into the Gulf of Mexico. It is about 2,340 miles long.

2. The **Rio Grande** begins in the San Juan Mountains of Colorado. It
   flows south, through New Mexico. Then it flows southeast along the
   Texas and Mexico border. It ends near Brownsville, Texas, where it
   flows into the Gulf of Mexico. It is about 1,760 miles long.

3. The **Susquehanna River** begins in New York state and flows south,
   ending in the Chesapeake Bay, northeast of Washington, D.C. It is
   about 447 miles long.

4. The **St. Lawrence River** begins at Lake Ontario and flows northeast
   through Canada. It ends in the Gulf of St. Lawrence, near the Atlan-
   tic Ocean. It is about 1,900 miles long.

5. The Great Lakes are five lakes on the northern border of the United
   States. **Lake Ontario** is on the far east, with a depth of 802 feet.
   Lake Erie is west and a bit south of Lake Ontario, with a depth of 210
   feet. **Lake Huron**, 750 feet deep, is north of Lake Erie. **Lake Michi-
   gan** is west of Lake Huron, with a depth of 923 feet. North of Lake
   Michigan is **Lake Superior**, with a depth of 1,330 feet.

6. The highest mountain in the U.S. is Mount McKinley, at 20,320 feet,
   in Alaska. (It is not on this map.) Other high mountains in the U.S.
   are: **Mt. Rainier**, near Seattle, at 14,410 feet; **Mt. Whitney**, in the
   Sierra Nevada Mountain Range in California, at 14,494 feet; **Mt.
   Elbert**, in Colorado, at 14,433 feet; **Mt. Washington**, in New Hamp-
   shire in the northeastern U.S., at 6,288 feet.

Name _____ Date _____

I **Map questions.** Write questions and answers about the map and information in exercise H on page 34. Use the cues given.
(Remember: Miles to kilometers = miles x 1.6. Feet to meters = feet x .3048.)

> **Example**
>
> how long / Rio Grande River   A: *How long is the Rio Grande River?*
>   B: *It's about 1,700 miles long.*

1. how long / Mississippi River _____

_____

2. how many kilometers / that _____

_____

3. where / Rio Grande River / begin _____

_____

4. where / Rio Grande River / end _____

_____

5. how high / Mt. McKinley _____

_____

6. how many meters / that _____

_____

7. how high / Mt. Washington _____

_____

8. how deep / Lake Erie _____

_____

9. how deep / Lake Superior _____

_____

10. what direction / St. Lawrence River / flow _____

_____

11. how long / St. Lawrence River _____

_____

12. how many kilometers / that _____

_____

13. where / Mississippi River / begin _____

_____

14. how long / Susquehanna River _____

_____

15. how high / Mt. Elbert _____

_____

16. how many meters / that _____

_____

© Heinle & Heinle Publishers. All rights reserved.

Asking about distance *(text, page 68)*

J **World distances.** Use information from the chart to write questions and answers about distances.

DISTANCES IN MILES			
From TO	**Cairo**	**Caracas**	**London**
Hong Kong	5,066	10,165	5,990
Madrid	2,087	4,346	785
Melbourne, Australia	8,675	9,717	10,500
New York	5,619	2,120	3,469

Example	
Hong Kong-Caracas	A: *How far is it from Hong Kong to Caracas?*
	B: *It's 10,165 miles.*

1. Hong Kong-London _____

_____

2. Melbourne-Cairo _____

_____

3. Caracas-Melbourne _____

_____

4. Madrid-Caracas _____

_____

5. New York-London _____

_____

6. New York-Caracas _____

_____

7. London-Melbourne _____

_____

8. Cairo-Madrid _____

_____

9. Caracas-Madrid _____

_____

10. Cairo-Hong Kong _____

_____

Final Activity

K **Write a letter.** Your friend is coming to visit you next weekend. You received this letter. Write a letter to your friend, suggesting places to visit and see. Tell where places are, too. Be sure to use correct friendly letter format: a salutation (Dear ...,), and a closing (Your friend,). Indent the first line of each new paragraph.

Dear _____ ,
   It was nice talking to you on the phone last night. I'm very excited about my trip. It will be great to see you again.
   I will be free on Friday afternoon and all day Saturday. I know you're busy Friday, but can you tell me where I should go? What is your city famous for? Are there any good museums or historical places? What is a good restaurant for dinner?
   On Saturday, let's do something together. Where should we go? Can we drive somewhere? Do you have a car? Maybe we can take a bus or train.
   I have to leave Saturday night. My flight is at 6:00 p.m.
   Please write to me with your suggestions.
                    Your friend,

                 _____

© Heinle & Heinle Publishers. All rights reserved.

I'm Going to Be Busy

Activities and chores *(text, page 73)*

A Weekend activities and chores. Check the activities and chores you do on the weekend.

Activities		Chores	
cook	——	clean your room	——
visit friends	——	help around the house	——
see a movie	——	go grocery shopping	——
practice something	——	work in the yard	——
go for long walks	——	fix things	——
sew	——	clean the kitchen	——
paint	——	wash windows	——
exercise	——	wash the car	——

B Questions and answers. Use information from exercise A to answer the questions. Add other chores and activities, too.

1. What activities do you like to do on the weekend?

_____

_____

_____

2. What chores do you usually do on the weekend?

_____

_____

_____

3. What chores are you going to do next weekend?

_____

_____

_____

4. What other activities are you going to do next weekend?

_____

_____

_____

Asking about plans and intentions *(text, page 74)*
Asking and telling about plans and intentions *(text, page 76)*

C Weekend plans. Ask three classmates about their weekend plans. Listen to their answers and take notes. You can use questions like the ones below.

Questions

What are you going to do this weekend?

What chores are you going to do?

Are you going to . . . ?

Example	
JUAN:	*visit friends Saturday night, watch TV, help brother fix car on Sunday, clean room*

1. _____
   _____
   _____

2. _____
   _____
   _____

3. _____
   _____
   _____

D Write about your classmates. Use the information from exercise C to write complete sentences about each classmate.

Example
Juan is going to visit friends on Saturday night. They are going to watch TV. On Sunday he's going to help his brother fix the car and he's going to clean his room.

1. _____
   _____
   _____

2. _____
   _____
   _____

3. _____
   _____
   _____

© Heinle & Heinle Publishers. All rights reserved.

E **What are your plans?** Write a paragraph about your plans for the weekend. Tell what you are going to do on Friday evening, Saturday morning, afternoon, and evening, and on Sunday. Give as many details as you can. Remember to indent the first line of the paragraph. Start you paragraph with one of these sentences: *I have many plans for the weekend* OR *I don't have many plans for the weekend.*

_____

_____

_____

_____

_____

_____

_____

_____

_____

F **Talk and rewrite.** Share your paragraph from exercise E with a partner. Let your partner read your paragraph and then talk about what you wrote. Does your partner have questions? Can you add more information to your paragraph? Did your partner find any mistakes? Can he or she help you correct them? After you discuss the paragraph with your partner, rewrite it below, making changes.

_____

_____

_____

_____

_____

_____

_____

_____

© Heinle & Heinle Publishers. All rights reserved.

Name _____   Date _____

Questions with *How often . . . ?* *(text, page 76)*

G **How often?** Use the cues to write questions. Then answer each question. (If you're in class, ask your partner these questions. If you're at home, answer them yourself.) In your answer, you can use *once, twice, three times, four times* (etc.), *a day, week, month, year; never.*

Example
(go to the dentist)
How often do you go to the dentist?   *Twice a year.*

1. (go for a long walk)

   _____   _____

2. (go to the doctor)

   _____   _____

3. (brush your teeth)

   _____   _____

4. (write a letter)

   _____   _____

5. (read a newspaper in English)

   _____   _____

6. (go to a movie)

   _____   _____

7. (eat in a restaurant)

   _____   _____

8. (exercise)

   _____   _____

9. (talk on the phone)

   _____   _____

10. (go grocery shopping)

   _____   _____

11. (visit a relative)

   _____   _____

12. (take an English test)

   _____   _____

Making predictions *(text, page 78)*

H What's your prediction? Look at each picture and write a prediction.

Example

Number 7 is going to win.

1. _____

2. _____

3. _____

4. _____

5. _____

6. _____

Expressing an opinion or giving advice *(text, page 79)*

I Give some advice. Write some advice for your friend who says the following things.

Example

"My room is a mess." *I think you should clean it.*

1. "I don't understand this lesson." _____

2. "I'm so tired." _____

3. "I lost my book in the library." _____

4. "I have a bad headache." _____

5. "I have three tests tomorrow." _____

6. "I need to relax." _____

7. "I want to learn to drive a car." _____

8. "I don't know how to swim." _____

9. "I don't have time to cook dinner." _____

10. "I want to speak English very well." _____

Asking for an opinion or advice with *I think*   (text, page 80)

J   **Advice and opinions.** Your friend is asking for your advice or opinion. Use the cues to write your friend's questions. Then answer them.

> **Example**
>
> where / go next summer
> YOUR FRIEND: *Where do you think I should go next summer?*
> YOU: *I think you should go to California.*

1. where / next summer

   YOUR FRIEND: _____

   YOU: _____

2. what record / buy

   YOUR FRIEND: _____

   YOU: _____

3. where / go to buy a good dictionary

   YOUR FRIEND: _____

   YOU: _____

4. what restaurant / go to for dinner

   YOUR FRIEND: _____

   YOU: _____

5. what class / take next semester

   YOUR FRIEND: _____

   YOU: _____

6. where / take a vacation next summer

   YOUR FRIEND: _____

   YOU: _____

7. when / study for the next English test

   YOUR FRIEND: _____

   YOU: _____

8. what sport / learn

   YOUR FRIEND: _____

   YOU: _____

9. what supermarket / shop at

   YOUR FRIEND: _____

   YOU: _____

10. where / go shopping for clothes

   YOUR FRIEND: _____

   YOU: _____

© Heinle & Heinle Publishers. All rights reserved.

K **Making plans in Boston.** Work with a partner. Imagine that you are visiting Boston. Look at the information about things to do in Boston. What do you think you should do? Where do you think you should go? Talk about plans, using the questions given. Be sure to check the weather report, too.

Places of Interest in Boston

Faneuil Hall Marketplace: Shops, restaurants, and boutiques in a famous old meeting hall
John F. Kennedy Library Museum: Displays and exhibits about the life and times of this famous president
Museum of Fine Arts: An excellent collection that includes a lot of Asian and European art. Coffee shops, restaurant, gift shop.
Museum of Science: Exhibits of natural history, physical science, medicine, and astronomy.
New England Aquarium: Circular glass tank containing more than 2000 fish and aquatic animals. Dolphin and sea lion shows daily.
U.S.S. Constitution: An old sailing ship from the U.S. Navy. Launched in Boston Harbor in 1797.
Freedom Trail Walking Tour: Half-day or full-day walking tour of the historic sites of Boston.

Weather Report
Saturday morning: clear. Saturday afternoon: rain.
Sunday morning: cloudy and cool. Sunday afternoon: sunny and cool.

Questions:
    What do you think I should see in Boston?
    Do you like museums / history / science / shopping / fish ?
    Do you think I should . . . ?

L **Write about it.** Write about what you are going to do on Saturday and Sunday. Use a pencil. Be sure to indent the first line of your paragraph.

_____

_____

_____

_____

_____

_____

_____

Now ask a classmate to read your paragraph. Does it make sense to him or her? Can he or she find any errors? Talk about your paragraph, and then make corrections.

Name _____ Date _____

Unit 8

Have a Good Flight!

Travel *(text, page 84)*

A **Word find.** There are twelve travel words hidden in the puzzle below. The words are down and across. Circle the twelve words. Then write the words on the lines.

X	O	F	L	I	G	H	T	V	B
S	E	A	T	N	U	M	B	E	R
A	C	T	H	U	O	B	K	A	E
I	F	R	I	A	T	A	S	G	B
R	J	I	P	Z	R	G	U	E	U
P	G	P	O	G	A	T	E	N	S
O	P	L	A	N	E	V	N	T	R
R	G	A	T	I	C	K	E	T	D
T	C	O	U	N	T	E	R	D	M

trip _____   _____

_____   _____

_____   _____

_____   _____

_____   _____

_____   _____

Travel *(text, page 84)*
Talking about past events *(text, page 85)*

B **Fill in the blanks.** Mrs. Fonseca is a saleswoman. She went to New York for business. Read about the end of her trip. Use the words from exercise A to complete the paragraph below.

    Mrs. Fonseca was worried about her (1) *trip* home. She left the office at 3:30,

and got on the (2) _____ to go to the airport. The traffic was terrible, so

she got to Kennedy International (3) _____ only 25 minutes before her

(4) _____ . She had her (5) _____ but had to go to the check-in

(6) _____ for a (7) _____ (8) _____ . There were many

people at the counter, but the (9) _____ worked quickly. The agent took

her (10) _____ and gave her a seat number. Then Mrs. Fonseca ran to the

(11) _____ . She boarded the (12) _____ , five minutes before flight

time. At 6:00 PM they closed the plane doors. She closed her eyes and finally relaxed.

She woke up at 9:00. Soon the plane landed. She was tired, but glad to be back!

© Heinle & Heinle Publishers. All rights reserved.

C **Past tense questions.** Write complete answers to the questions, using information from the story in exercise B on page 45.

1. What time did Mrs. Fonseca leave the office? _____

2. Did she take a taxi to the airport? _____

3. Did she get to the airport early? Why or why not? _____

    _____

4. Where did she go first, to the check-in counter or the gate? _____

    _____

5. What did she have to get at the counter? _____

6. Did she walk to the gate? _____

7. When did they close the plane doors? _____

8. Did she read a book on the plane? _____

9. When did she wake up? _____

10. Her flight from New York was about three hours long. Where do you think she went?

    _____

D **Your turn.** Write about a trip you took. Was it a short trip or a long trip? Where did you go? How did you get there? Tell about your trip, giving details.

_____

_____

_____

_____

E **Past tense review.** Do you remember the simple present and simple past tense forms of these irregular verbs? Fill in the missing forms in the list below.

Simple present form	Simple past form	Simple present form	Simple past form
go	_went_	get	_____
see	_____	_____	bought
_____	made	meet	_____
have to	_____	be	_____
_____	drove	_____	flew
take	_____	leave	_____

Name _____ Date _____

F **Ask your partner.** Use the verbs from exercise E, page 46, to write past tense questions to ask a partner. Your questions can start with: *Did, What, When, What time, Where, How, How many.*

1. _____ ?

2. _____ ?

3. _____ ?

4. _____ ?

5. _____ ?

6. _____ ?

7. _____ ?

8. _____ ?

9. _____ ?

10. _____ ?

G **Partner's answers.** Now trade papers with a partner. Your partner will write answers to your questions from exercise F and you will write answers to your partner's questions.

1. _____

2. _____

3. _____

4. _____

5. _____

6. _____

7. _____

8. _____

9. _____

10. _____

© Heinle & Heinle Publishers. All rights reserved.

Information questions: *how long* and *who* *(direct object)* *(text, page 86)*

H **Mrs. Fonseca's visit to New York.** Yesterday Mrs. Fonseca was in New York City on business. She was at Imports International in the morning, and stayed there for lunch. Then she went to Intex Sales Company in the afternoon. Look at her schedule from yesterday. Today she is in her office and her boss, Ms. Brown, has many questions for her. Write the questions and answers, using the cues given.

Example
who / see at breakfast
MS. BROWN: *Who did you see at breakfast?*
MRS. FONSECA: *I saw Mr. Tanaka.*

FRIDAY
New York Schedule
7:00- 8:30 *have breakfast with Mr. Tanaka at Imports International*
8:45-10:00 *meet with Ms. Carrera and Mr. Munoz*
10:15-12:15 *see Mr. Roding*
12:30- 2:00 *have lunch with Ms. Carrera*
2:30-3:30 *visit Mrs. Thompson at Intex Sales Co.*

1. how long / meet with Mr. Tanaka

MS. BROWN: _____

MRS. FONSECA: _____

2. who / meet with next

MS. BROWN: _____

MRS. FONSECA: _____

3. how long / talk with them

MS. BROWN: _____

MRS. FONSECA: _____

4. who / see after that

MS. BROWN: _____

MRS. FONSECA: _____

5. how long / meet with him

MS. BROWN: _____

MRS. FONSECA: _____

6. who / talk with at lunch

MS. BROWN: _____

MRS. FONSECA: _____

7. how long / talk with her

MS. BROWN: _____

MRS. FONSECA: _____

8. who / visit in the afternoon

MS. BROWN: _____

MRS. FONSECA: _____

Name _____   Date _____

Time expression + *ago*   *(text, page 88)*

I   **Personal questions.** Write answers using *ago*.

1. When were you born? _____

2. When did you start to study English? _____

3. When did you start to use this book? _____

4. When did you start to do this exercise? _____

5. When did you have something to eat? _____

6. When did you wake up today? _____

7. When did you take a vacation? _____

8. When did you have your last English test? _____

Making and responding to polite requests (1) *(text, page 89)*
Making and responding to polite requests (2) *(text, page 90)*

J   **Polite requests.** Read each situation and write a request and a response. Use *Could* I or *Could you*. Respond with *Yes, of course, Sure,* or *I'm afraid . . . .*

> **Example**
>
> You need someone to give you a piece of paper.
> A: *Could you give me a piece of paper, please?*
> B: *Sure. Here you are.*

1. You need to use a telephone book.

   A: _____

   B: _____

2. You need someone to give you fifty cents.

   A: _____

   B: _____

3. You need to use a friend's pencil.

   A: _____

   B: _____

4. You need someone to explain a math problem to you.

   A: _____

   B: _____

5. You want to read a friend's newspaper.

   A: _____

   B: _____

© Heinle & Heinle Publishers. All rights reserved.

K A dream trip. Imagine that you can take a trip to any place in the world for one week. You can take one friend with you, and you have as much money as you need. Think about where you are going to go on your dream trip, what you are going to see, what you are going to do, etc. Write answers to the questions to help you plan your trip.

1. Where are you going to go? _____

2. Why do you want to go there? _____

3. Who is going to go with you? _____

4. What do you want to do there? _____

5. Are you going to see anyone you know there? _____

6. Are you going to visit any famous places? _____

7. Are you going to buy anything special? _____

L Talk about it. Work together with a partner. Tell your partner all about the dream trip you are going to take. Answer any questions your partner has. Then talk with your partner about his or her dream trip.

M Write about it. Now imagine that you already took your dream trip. Write a paragraph about what happened on the trip. Use the past tense. Give as many details as you can. When you are finished, check your writing for any mistakes. Then share your paragraph with your partner. Can your partner help you make any more corrections?

_____

_____

_____

_____

_____

_____

_____

_____

_____

_____

_____

Unit 9 — I'm Bored with My Job

Expressing dissatisfaction *(text, page 95)*

A **What's the matter?** Write a conversation between you and a friend. You don't look happy. Your friend asks what the matter is. You answer, using the cues and *bored with* or *tired of.* Then your friend makes a suggestion. Choose a suggestion from the list to complete the conversation, or write a suggestion of your own.

Suggestions

Ex   Why don't you listen to a different record?

____   Why don't you look for a new job?

____   Why don't you buy a new jacket?

____   Why don't you cook something else?

____   Why don't you go to the library and get a different one?

____   Why don't you watch a different program?

> **Example**
>
> bored / music A: *What's the matter?*
> B: *I guess I'm bored with this music.*
> A: *Why don't you listen to a different record?*

1. tired / food   A: _____
                    B: _____
                    A: _____

2. bored / TV program A: _____
                    B: _____
                    A: _____

3. tired / jacket   A: _____
                    B: _____
                    A: _____

4. bored / job   A: _____
                    B: _____
                    A: _____

5. bored / book   A: _____
                    B: _____
                    A: _____

© Heinle & Heinle Publishers. All rights reserved.

More occupations *(text, pages 96-97)*
Contrasting would *like to + verb* with *like to + verb* *(text, page 97)*

B **Occupations and interests.** Read what each person likes to do. Then guess what the person would like to be, choosing an occupation from the list. Write sentences about each person, following the example. In numbers 10-12, write about yourself and people you know.

Occupations: flight attendant / cook / waitress / nurse / actress / mechanic / home-maker / travel agent / computer programmer / electrician / bank teller / lawyer / firefighter / farmer / carpenter / journalist / letter carrier / secretary / receptionist

Example
John / work with computers
John likes to work with computers. He would like to be a computer programmer.

1. Marie / walk, see people

_____

2. Peter / fix cars

_____

3. Susan / dance, sing, and act

_____

4. Yoshi / travel, help people

_____

5. Vinh / help people, study science and health

_____

6. Rosa / work with people, do math

_____

7. Anna / fix radios, TVs

_____

8. Thomas / interview people, write

_____

9. May / prepare meals, bake

_____

10. (you)

_____

11. (a relative)

_____

12. (a friend)

_____

Asking for additional information *(text, page 98)*

C **What else can you do?** Fill in the first line of the conversation with something about yourself. Then complete the conversation, following the example. Use your imagination, if necessary.

> **Example**
>
> A: I play *tennis*.
> B: *What else do you play?*
> A: *I play baseball, too.*

1. A: I can cook_____.   4. A: I play _____. *(sport, game, music)*
   B: _____   B: _____
   A: _____   A: _____

2. A: I like to watch _____.   5. A: I like to _____.
   B: _____   B: _____
   A: _____   A: _____

3. A: I bought _____.   6. A: I can speak_____.
   B: _____   B: _____
   A: _____   A: _____

Talking about ability *(text, page 100)*

D **Complete the conversation.** Mike Lee is going to graduate from high school in June. He can't decide what he wants to do. His teacher is trying to help him. Fill in the blanks with *want to, like to, like, know,* or *know how to.*

MR. PEREZ:	Do you _____ go to college?
MIKE:	Yes, but I don't _____ what I want to study.
MR. PEREZ:	What do you _____ be?
MIKE:	I don't _____ .
MR. PEREZ:	What do you _____ study in school?
MIKE:	I _____ study math. I also _____ foreign languages, but I don't _____ speak any very well.
MR. PEREZ:	What do you _____ do at home?
MIKE:	I _____ work with machines and I _____ play computer games.
MR. PEREZ:	Do you _____ fix things?
MIKE:	Yes. I _____ fix cars, bikes, and small engines.
MR. PEREZ:	Hmmm . . . math, computer games, and machines. Do you _____ study computer science?
MIKE:	No. I don't _____ be a programmer.
MR. PEREZ:	Then maybe engineering is the subject for you.

© Heinle & Heinle Publishers. All rights reserved.

Describing personal qualities *(text, page 101)*

E **Write about yourself.** Read the list of vocabulary from the unit. Next read the sentences explaining new words to describe personal qualities. Then write short descriptions about yourself, a friend, and a family member. Write all the good things you can. Don't be shy! Add details, too.

Vocabulary: caring / outgoing / careful / patient / creative / energetic

Some new vocabulary:

a. A *strong* person can lift and carry big things.

b. A *friendly* person is nice to other people.

c. An *artistic* person is very creative.

d. A *studious* person studies a lot.

e. A *helpful* person enjoys helping other people.

f. A *musical* person can play an instrument or sing well.

g. A *pleasant* or *cheerful* person is happy, nice, and helpful.

Example
My father is musical. He plays the guitar and sings. He is helpful and outgoing. He always helps our neighbors when they need it.

About yourself

_____

_____

About a friend

_____

_____

About a family member

_____

_____

Name _____   Date _____

F **Interviews.** Interview your classmates about what their interests are, what they know how to do, and what job they would like to have. Ask them about their personal qualities. First, fill in the information about yourself. Then interview two classmates. If you're not in class, interview two friends or family members. Fill in the chart with your notes.

	You	_____	_____
What do you like to do?			
What do you know how to do?			
What job would you like to have?			
Why would you like to have that job?			
Tell me about yourself. (Personal qualities)			

© Heinle & Heinle Publishers. All rights reserved.

G **Write about it.** Use the information from your chart on page 55. Write a paragraph about yourself, and one paragraph about each classmate. Be sure to indent the first line of each paragraph. You can add any additional details or information you know.

1. _____

_____

_____

_____

_____

_____

2. _____

_____

_____

_____

_____

_____

_____

3. _____

_____

_____

_____

_____

_____

Name _____   Date _____

Interviews and résumés *(text, page 106)*

A **Fill in the blanks.** Use the vocabulary below to complete the paragraph. You will use some words more than once.

Vocabulary: applicants / appointment / education / experience / interview / job ad / manager / résumés / salesperson

Mr. Salerno is a (1) _____ at Warner's Department Store in

Winfield. Yesterday he put a (2) _____ in the newspaper for a

(3) _____ to sell suits in the men's department. The ad said that

(4) _____ should send their (5) _____ to him.

This morning, he received five (6) _____ in the mail. He read

them and then called three of the (7) _____ . He made an

(8) _____ for each one to come in for an (9) _____

at the store tomorrow. He will ask them more about their (10) _____ ,

(11) _____ , and interests.

B **Don Penn's résumé.** Don Penn read the ad for a job at Warner's Department Store. He is preparing his résumé. Put his information on the correct lines of the résumé on page 58. Look at the résumé on page 106 of your text for an example. Be sure to print neatly. Don't forget capital letters, commas, and periods.

• 1986 - 1990   Winfield High School, Winfield, NY

• 1988 - 1990   Cashier for Bell's Supermarket, Winfield, NY

• Good Spanish

• Summer 1990   Kitchen assistant at Mountain Hotel, Lake George, NY

• 1990 - present   Winfield Community College, Winfield, NY

• Prof. Carleton, Math Department, Winfield Community College

• 1990 - present   Cashier at Calese's Quick Mart, Winfield, NY

• Katherine Johnson, Mountain Hotel, Lake George, NY

• Don Penn

• Vito Calese, Calese's Quick Mart Winfield, NY

• 77 School Street

• Winfield, NY

© Heinle & Heinle Publishers. All rights reserved.

Résumé

Don Penn

_____

_____

Phone: 599-4872

Education

_____   _____

             _____

_____   _____

             _____

Experience

_____   _____

             _____

_____   _____

             _____

_____   _____

             _____

Languages   _____

References   _____

                   _____

                   _____

                   _____

                   _____

                   _____

                   _____

                   _____

Name _____   Date _____

Prepositions: *from . . . until . . .*   *(text, page 107)*

C   **Your turn.** Write true answers, using *from . . . until . . .*, to these questions about yourself.

> **Example**
> When did you sleep last night? *I slept from 11:00 until 6:30.*

1. When did you sleep last night? _____
2. When did you study or work yesterday? _____
3. When did you eat dinner yesterday? _____
4. When did you go to class yesterday (or last week)? _____
5. When did you go to elementary school? _____

D   **About your life.** Write five sentences about your life using *from . . . until.* For example, you can write about where you studied before now, where you lived before you moved to your present home, where you worked before, when you went on vacation, etc.

1. _____
2. _____
3. _____
4. _____
5. _____

E   **Recent United States presidents.** Look at the information in the chart. Then write sentences about each president, using *from . . . until.*

Dwight D. Eisenhower	1953-1961
John F. Kennedy	1961-1963
Lyndon B. Johnson	1963-1969
Richard M. Nixon	1969-1974
Gerald R. Ford	1974-1977
James E. Carter	1977-1981
Ronald Reagan	1981-1989

> **Example**
> *Dwight D. Eisenhower was president from 1953 until 1961.*

1. _____
2. _____
3. _____
4. _____
5. _____
6. _____

© Heinle & Heinle Publishers. All rights reserved.

Preposition: *during* (*text, page 108*)

F **When did it happen?** Look at the picture and the words. Write a question and an answer, using *during*.

Example

Sheila / sleep
When did Sheila sleep?
She slept during the movie.

1.

Alan / meet / Sylvie

_____

_____

2.

Sue and Ellen / excited

_____

_____

3.

Tom / bored

_____

_____

4.

Jim / busy

_____

_____

5.

Ruth /drop her keys

_____

_____

G **Preposition review.** Complete the sentences about Don with *in, on, at, to, during, from,* or *until.* Use information from Don's résumé on page 58, exercise B.

1. Don lives _____ 77 School Street _____ Winfield.

2. He went _____ Winfield High School _____ 1986 _____ 1990.

3. Now he is a cashier _____ Calese's Quick Mart _____ Winfield.

4. He started to work _____ Calese's Quick Mart _____ 1990.

5. _____ the summer of 1990, he worked _____ the Mountain Hotel.

6. He goes _____ Winfield Community College _____ night. His classes are _____ Monday and Wednesday.

7. He was a cashier at Bell's Supermarket _____ 1988 _____ 1990.

8. He started to study _____ the community college _____ 1990.

9. He met Professor Carleton _____ his first semester _____ the community college.

10. Vito Calese works _____ Calese's Quick Mart. The store is _____ Main Street.

Reporting what someone said *(text, page 110)*

H **Don's interview.** Match what Mr. Salerno said in the interview and Don's response.

Mr. Salerno

1. "You don't have department store experience."
2. "We have many Spanish-speaking customers."
3. "The hours are from 12 to 5, Thursday through Sunday."
4. "You have to learn how to use a cash register."
5. "Sometimes employees work on holidays."
6. "The salary is $7.25 an hour."
7. "I want to offer you the job."

Don

____ a. "That's OK. I work some holidays at the gas station."

____ b. "I know how to use a cash register."

____ c. "That's fine. I like to speak Spanish."

____ d. "That's true, but I am outgoing and I like to work with people."

____ e. "That's OK. My classes are on Monday and Wednesday nights."

____ f. "Thank you. I really want to work here."

____ g. "That sounds good."

I **Write about the interview.** Write what Mr. Salerno said and what Don said to Mr. Salerno. Start with number 1 in exercise G.

1. *Mr. Salerno said Don doesn't* _____

   Don said he _____

2. _____

   _____

3. _____

   _____

4. _____

   _____

5. _____

   _____

6. _____

   _____

7. _____

   _____

© Heinle & Heinle Publishers. All rights reserved.

J   **Role play.** Work with a partner to role play an interview between Mr. Salerno and Don Penn. If you want, you can change their names to Mrs. Salerno and Donna Penn. Use information from page 57, page 58, and page 61. Be sure to include the steps below and use some of the questions suggested. Perform the role play two times, changing roles.

1. Introductions
2. Mr. Salerno's questions:

   How long did you . . . ?   Why . . . ?

   How long were you . . . ?   What . . . ?

   When did / were/ you . . . ?   Tell me about . . .

3. Mr. Salerno gives information about the job.
4. Don asks a question.
5. Don thanks Mr. Salerno for the interview and says good-bye.

K   **Write the conversation.** Write out the interview that you performed with your partner. Use as many lines as you need.

MR. SALERNO: _____

DON: _____

MR. SALERNO: _____

DON: _____

MR. SALERNO: _____

DON: _____

MR. SALERNO: _____

DON: _____

MR. SALERNO: _____

DON: _____

MR. SALERNO: _____

DON: _____

MR. SALERNO: _____

DON: _____

MR. SALERNO: _____

DON: _____

MR. SALERNO: _____

DON: _____

Unit 11 They Lost the Game!

Talking about sports *(text, page 115)*

A **Conversations about sports.** Complete the conversations below, using the vocabulary listed. Be sure to put verbs in the correct form. Use some words more than once.

Vocabulary: athlete / fast / go to bed / kick / match / pretty / race / team / win / hard

1. A: What are you going to do tonight?
   B: I'm going to study and _____ at 9:30.
   A: Why are you going to _____ so early?
   B: I have a big tennis _____ tomorrow afternoon, so I need a lot of rest.
2. A: Did you watch the swimming _____ on TV yesterday?
   B: No, I had to work. Who _____ ?
   A: The _____ from France. They were great!
3. A: Is Ted a good _____ ?
   B: Yes, he's _____ good. He's on the swim _____
   and the soccer _____ .
   A: Is he a good soccer player?
   B: Yes. He runs _____ and _____ the ball
   _____ .

B **Thinking about sports.** Write answers to these questions.

1. What sports do you like to play or do? Why? _____
   _____
2. What sports do you like to watch? Why? _____
3. Do you watch sports on TV? What sports? _____

C **Write about sports.** Think of a topic or choose one of the topics listed below. Then write a short paragraph, using ideas from exercise B. After you are finished, exchange papers with a classmate. Read each other's paragraphs. Can you help each other make corrections?

Topics:
Sports I Like to Play
Sports I Like to Watch
Why I Don't Like Sports
Team Sports at My School

_____
_____
_____
_____

© Heinle & Heinle Publishers. All rights reserved.

Giving sports results: simple past of irregular verbs: *come, win, lose, beat* (text, page 115)

D **Sports Day.** Each May in Winfield, high school sports teams have basketball, volleyball, and soccer matches and track events. Look at the results from this year's Sports Day. Write sentences, using the cues and information from the chart.

THIRD ANNUAL SPORTS DAY   Central High vs. West High
CH = Central High   WH = West High

Track Events	Basketball	Volleyball
100 Yard Dash	Girls' CH 68	Boys' and Girls' Teams
Girls' 1st Connie Lin, CH	WH 51	WH 3
2nd Alice Poulot, CH	Boys' CH 73	CH 1
3rd Marie Cordon, WH	WH 71	
Boys' 1st Tom Wilson, WH		
2nd Vinh Tran, CH	**Soccer**	
3rd Jose Gomez, WH	Girls' WH 3	
Relay Race	CH 1	
Girls' CH	Boys' CH 1	
Boys' WH	WH 1	

Example
Connie Lin / girls' 100 yard dash   *Connie Lin won the girls' 100 yard dash*.

1. Alice Poulot / came in

_____

2. Tom Wilson / won

_____

3. Jose Gomez / came in

_____

4. Central High / relay race

_____

5. West High's, girls' basketball team / 68 to 51

_____

6. Central High's, boys' basketball team / 73 to 71

_____

7. West High's, girls' soccer team / beat / 3 to 1

_____

8. Central High's, girls' soccer team / match with West High

_____

9. West High's boys' soccer

_____

10. volleyball

_____

Name _____ Date _____

Object pronouns: *me, us, them* *(text, page 117)*

E **Complete the conversation.** Jose and Pete are talking about Sports Day. (See exercise D, page 64.) They are students at Central High. Fill in the blanks with *me, us, them.*

JOSE: That was a great basketball game, wasn't it? It was close, but we beat _____ .

PETE: Yeah. The girls' team won, too. Hey, why didn't you go to the volleyball match with _____ ?

JOSE: Oh, Connie invited _____ to see her run in the 100 yard dash.

PETE: Really? How did she do?

JOSE: She came in first. She always wins. She's fantastic. Who won the boys' soccer?

PETE: It was a tie. And the girls' soccer team beat _____ 3 to 1. How about the relay races?

JOSE: I didn't see _____ , but Connie told _____ the girls' team won. West High's boys' relay team beat _____ .

PETE: I guess the boys' teams didn't do very well this year. Maybe next year we will beat _____ in everything.

JOSE: Yeah! Hey, why don't you come with _____ to the snack bar? I'm hungry.

PETE: Sure. Since you invited _____ , you can buy _____ something.

JOSE: Now wait a minute . . .

Describing someone's abilities *(text, pages 118-119)*

F **People's abilities.** Look at the vocabulary below. Write sentences about people's abilities. You can write about yourself, classmates, friends, family members, or famous people.

Vocabulary:

runner	BUT	soccer	
swimmer		chess	
skier		volleyball	
dancer		tennis	player
singer		baseball	
ice skater		basketball	

very poor / poor / fair / good / very good / excellent

Example

My friend Alicia is an excellent dancer.

1. _____
2. _____
3. _____
4. _____
5. _____
6. _____
7. _____
8. _____
9. _____
10. _____

© Heinle & Heinle Publishers. All rights reserved.

Describing how people do things *(text, page 120)*

G **Your turn.** Say if you like to do the following things and tell how well you do them. In your answer, you can use these words: *well, badly, quickly, slowly, beautifully.*

Example	
dance?	*I don't like to dance, and I dance badly.*
OR	*I like to dance, and I dance very well.*
OR	*I like to dance, but I dance badly.*

1. dance?

   _____

2. speak English?

   _____

3. cook?

   _____

4. run?

   _____

5. play *(sport or musical instrument)*?

   _____

6. sing?

   _____

7. draw?

   _____

8. ice skate?

   _____

9. swim?

   _____

10. drive a car?

   _____

H **People you know.** Write about five people you know who do things very well.

Example
My sister Michele plays soccer very well.

1. _____
2. _____
3. _____
4. _____
5. _____

Name _____ Date _____

As . . . as possible (text, page 121)

I **What's your advice?** Imagine that a friend is moving from your native country to live in the United States. What is your advice? Write suggestions using *You should, You have to,* and *as . . . as possible.*

1. study English / much *You should study English as* _____

2. listen to English / carefully _____

3. practice speaking English / much _____

4. use your English / often _____

5. read English newspapers / often _____

6. ask your English-speaking friends to be / patient _____

_____

Final Activities

J **Getting ready to write a letter.** Write a letter to a friend who is moving from your native country to the United States. If you are not living in the United States now, imagine that a friend is moving from the United States to your country. First, write down some notes about what you are going to say in your letter by answering the questions below.

1. Do you think your friend is going to like your city or town? Why or why not?

   Describe interesting places in and near your city or town. _____

   _____

2. What's the weather like? _____

   _____

3. What is your advice for your friend? How can he or she learn the language? Use some

   ideas from exercise I and add your own ideas. _____

   _____

4. What would you like your friend to bring or send you from his or her country? Is there

   something special you would like? _____

   _____

5. Other things you want to mention in your letter, such as clothes your friend should

   bring: _____

   _____

   _____

© Heinle & Heinle Publishers. All rights reserved.

K **Write your letter.** Use your notes from exercise J to write your letter. You may want to use some of these expressions: *you should, I think you should, would like, could you, have to, like to.*

Use correct letter format. In letters, you write your street address, town and state, and the date (for example, January 15, 1992) on the three lines at the top right. Then write the salutation (*Dear* _____ ,) on the top line on the left. Be sure to indent the first line of each paragraph. For your closing, use *Yours truly, Sincerely, Your friend,* or *Love.* Then sign your name on the line under the closing.

After you finish writing, go back and check your work. Look for correct punctuation (periods, commas, question marks) and capitalization. You may want to exchange letters with a classmate and read each other's letter.

_____

(street address)

_____

(city, state, country)

_____

(today's date)

_____

(salutation)

_____

_____

_____

_____

_____

_____

_____

_____

_____

_____

_____

_____

_____

(closing)

_____

(signature)

Name _____ Date _____

Unit 12 | I Wish I Could . . .

Object pronouns: *him* and *her* *(text, page 127)*

A **Him or her?** Complete the sentences with the correct form of the verb and *him* or *her*.

> **Example**
>
> (like) Sarah often visits Mary after work. Sarah *likes her* very much.

1. (love) Sarah's boyfriend is Thomas. She _____ very much.
2. (talk with) Sarah called Thomas last night and _____ for about 20 minutes.
3. (admire) Sarah thinks Steffi Graf is an excellent athlete. She really _____ .
4. (write to) Sarah has a British friend named Elizabeth. She _____ every month.
5. (visit) Sarah's uncle lives a few miles away. She _____ on the weekend.
6. (laugh at) Her uncle is very funny and she always _____ .
7. (give) Sarah went to her uncle's birthday party last Saturday. She _____ a shirt.
8. (play with) Sarah likes to play basketball with her sister. Sometimes she _____ on Sunday.

B **Complete the conversation.** This is a phone conversation between Sarah and Ana. Sarah is inviting Ana to her house to make ice cream. Complete the conversation with these words: *I, me, my, we, us, our, you, your, it, its, he, him, his, she, her, they, them, their.* You do not have to use all the words.

SARAH: Hi, Ana. Are _____ busy?

ANA: Yes, _____ am. I'm having problems with _____ car and I have to take _____ to the mechanic.

SARAH: Oh, that's too bad. _____ 'm calling because everybody's here at _____ house. _____ 're going to make ice cream. Do you want to come over and help _____ ?

ANA: Sure! But first _____ have to take the car to the mechanic. I talked with _____ this morning, and _____ said it was a quick job. So, who is there at the house with _____ ?

SARAH: Thomas and his brother are here. _____ brought a good recipe and also _____ new ice cream maker.

ANA: Oh, you are making me hungry!

SARAH: OK. Come as soon as you can. _____ is going to be ready in an hour.

ANA: Great! But don't eat it all before _____ get there!

© Heinle & Heinle Publishers. All rights reserved.

Comparing how people do things *(text, page 129)*

C **Comparing.** Compare the people in the pictures, using the words given. Use *as . . . as* or *not as . . . as.*

Example

(late)

Tom is as late as Allen.

1. (fast)

4. (hard)

_____

_____

2. (beautifully)

5. (late)

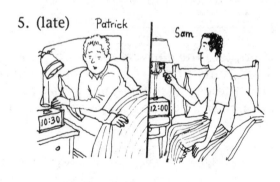
_____

_____

3. (early)

6. (much)

_____

_____

D **Your turn.** Write about yourself and people you know. Write true sentences with *as . . . as* or *not as . . . as,* using the cues. For numbers 9 and 10, make up your own sentences.

Example
sleep / much   *I don't sleep as much as my brother Bill.*

1. sleep / much   _____
2. go to bed / late   _____
3. eat / much   _____
4. study / hard   _____
5. play ___ / well   _____
6. run / fast   _____
7. get up / late   _____
8. speak English / well   _____
9. _____   _____
10. _____   _____

Comparing people and places *(text, page 130)*

E Questions for a partner. Write questions for a partner to answer, following the example. Then exchange papers. You write answers to your partner's questions, and your partner will write answers to your questions.

Example
Where / go *Where would you like to go? San Francisco or Los Angeles?* *I'd like to go to San Francisco. Los Angeles isn't as interesting as San Francisco.*

1. Where / go

_____

_____

2. Who / meet

_____

_____

3. Where / live

_____

_____

4. What movie / see

_____

_____

5. What job / have

_____

_____

© Heinle & Heinle Publishers. All rights reserved.

Expressing and explaining wishes and desires *(text, page 132)*

F **Your wishes.** What are your wishes? Answer the questions.

> **Example**
>
> Where do you wish you could be right now? Why?
> *I wish I could be on a beautiful, warm beach because I'm tired of cold weather.*

1. Where do you wish you could be right now? Why?_____

_____

2. What do you wish you could do? Why? _____

_____

3. Who do you wish you could see? Why? _____

_____

4. What do you wish you could have? Why? _____

_____

G **Two wishes.** Imagine that you could have two wishes come true. You can wish for any two things you want. Write a paragraph about what two things you wish for and why. After you finish, share your writing with your classmates.

_____

_____

_____

_____

_____

_____

_____

H **Classmates' wishes.** What did your classmates wish for in exercise G? Write about what they wish.

> **Example**
>
> *Martin wishes he could . . .*

1. _____

2. _____

3. _____

4. _____

5. _____

Name _____ Date _____

Making an inference *(text, page 133)*

I **Vocabulary review.** Look at the list of adjectives to describe people. Find a word in the vocabulary list that means the opposite and write it in the blank.

Vocabulary: awful / early / short / big / boring / busy / happy / fast

1. late _____

2. slow _____

3. interesting _____

4. bored _____

5. small _____

6. sad _____

7. tall _____

8. wonderful _____

J **You must be . . .** Write a response in each conversation, using *must be.* Use each of the following words once: *strong, tired, late, bored, busy, happy, sick, proud, excited, cold.*

> **Example**
> A: I stayed up until 12:00 last night.
> B: *You must be very tired.*

1. A: Our team won the game 3-0.

   B: _____

2. A: My job is the same every day.

   B: _____

3. A: I have a fever and a headache.

   B: _____

4. A: I forgot my sweater.

   B: _____

5. A: I spent all day cleaning my house.

   B: _____

6. A: My brother won his last race.

   B: _____

7. A: My sister is getting married next week.

   B: _____

8. A: It's 9:05 and Ernesto isn't here. Where is he?

   B: _____

9. A: I have something I have to do every night this week.

   B: _____

10. A: Sally carried those big boxes into the house.

    B: _____

© Heinle & Heinle Publishers. All rights reserved.

K **Interview.** In the Final Activity in your text (page 137), you talked with a classmate about wishes and desires. Now you are going to use some of the same questions to interview one of your teachers. Ask the questions below and write down notes as you listen to your teacher's answers. You can work with a partner if you want.

1. Imagine that you can't be a teacher (or other occupation). What would you like to be? Why?

_____

_____

2. Which famous people do you wish you could meet? Why?

_____

_____

3. Who do you admire? Why?

_____

_____

4. Imagine you could live anywhere in the world. Where would you like to live? Why?

_____

_____

5. You can have two wishes that are going to come true. What do you wish? Why?

_____

_____

L **Write about your interview.** Use your notes from exercise K. Write a paragraph about your interview. After, ask your partner to read your paragraph. Did he or she find any mistakes?

_____

_____

_____

_____

_____

_____

_____

_____

_____

_____

Unit 13 — What Happened to Sam?

Who and what questions with two-word verbs *(text, page 139)*

A **Fill in the blanks.** Complete the sentences using the vocabulary. You may use verbs more than once. Use the correct tense and form of the verb.

Vocabulary: wait for / look for / speak to / write to / worry about / think about / look at / forget about / listen to

1. Don't _____ our math test! It's tomorrow and you have to study.
2. Sofia _____ her mother in Colombia every week. Her letters are usually long and interesting.
3. Mrs. Wilson always _____ her son. He does poorly in school and is bored at home.
4. We _____ the bus for 20 minutes last night. It came at 10:30!
5. "You need to _____ your plans for next year. What courses are you going to take?"
6. Amanda went to the library. She _____ a book about French art history, but she didn't find one.
7. Chris loves to _____ rock and roll music.
8. My friend and I are going shopping. We are going to _____ shoes.
9. She was so angry at her boyfriend that she didn't want to _____ him on the phone.
10. "What do you _____ my new sweater? Do you like it?"

B **Questions.** A friend asks you questions. Use the cues to write each conversation.

> **Example**
>
> who / like to talk to / phone
> A: *Who do you like to talk to on the phone?*
> B: *I like to talk to Ellen and Marie.*

1. who / like to talk to / phone
   A: _____
   B: _____
2. what / talk about / with friends
   A: _____
   B: _____
3. what radio station / listen to
   A: _____
   B: _____
4. what / think about / in your free time
   A: _____
   B: _____
5. what / sometimes / worry about
   A: _____
   B: _____

© Heinle & Heinle Publishers. All rights reserved.

Nouns as adjective *(text, page 141)*

C **Matching nouns.** Match each noun on the left with a pair of nouns on the right. Then write out the words, using the noun as an adjective.

> **Example**
>
> accident *e. car accident, train accident*

1. music _____
2. player _____
3. class _____
4. coach _____
5. worker _____
6. chair _____

a. English, math

b. kitchen, dining room

c. factory, office

d. soccer, guitar

e. car, train

f. rock, piano

g. tennis, basketball

D **Sentences.** Use five pairs of words from exercise C to write sentences.

> **Example**
>
> *I saw a car accident last week.*

1. _____
2. _____
3. _____
4. _____
5. _____

Possessive of plural nouns *(text, page 142)*

E **Punctuation practice.** Add apostrophes and periods to the paragraph. Underline letters that should be capitalized.

Central High Sports News

during last nights girls basketball game, there was an accident with three players two girls from central high ran into west highs sandra jones all three girls fell jones hurt her knee sandras knee was x-rayed at the hospital this was sandras first injury of the season cindy wilson, captain of centrals girls basketball team, hurt her shoulder, but not badly she returned to the game in the second quarter and continued her high scoring center guard marie esteban of west high hurt her ankle her coach was worried about estebans injury, but it did not seem serious both coaches asked for time out the game started again after a few minutes the girls accident did not stop the excitement of the game the crowd cheered loudly until the end, when west high broke the tie the final score was 78-79 this was west highs fifth win of the season

Identifying body parts and injuries *(text, page 144)*
Talking about accidents and health problems *(text, page 145)*

F **Questions about the game.** Look back at the paragraph in exercise E and answer these questions about the game.

1. What happened during last night's girls' basketball game?

_____

2. What happened to Sandra Jones?

_____

3. Did she hurt her leg?

_____

4. Did she go to the hospital?

_____

5. What did Cindy Jones hurt?

_____

6. How did she hurt it?

_____

7. Did she hurt it badly?

_____

8. What team does Marie Esteban play on?

_____

9. What happened to her?

_____

10. Did she hurt it badly?

_____

11. What was her coach worried about?

_____

12. Was it an exciting game?

_____

13. Did West High lose the game?

_____

14. What was the final score?

_____

© Heinle & Heinle Publishers. All rights reserved.

G **Vocabulary.** Read each clue and write the part of the body.

1. You think with this. _ _ _ _d_

2. A tennis player needs a strong . . . . _w_ _ _ _ _

3. If you eat too much food, this may hurt. _ _ _ _m_ _ _ _

4. You may hurt this if you lift something too heavy. _ _ _ _ _

5. These are very important to a runner. _ _ _ _

6. If these are not good, you wear glasses. _ _ _ _

7. These are important for a guitar player or a piano player. _ _ _ _ _ _ _

8. This is the part of your leg right above the foot and below the knee. _ _ _ _ _

9. In a car accident, an injury to this is very serious. _n_ _ _ _

10. When you wear sandals, you can see these. _ _ _ _s_

H **Your experience.** Write a paragraph about an injury or sickness you had. Decide which you will write about, and then use the questions below to help you organize your ideas. Write down some notes. Then write your paragraph, giving as many details as you can.

Injury   OR **Sickness**

1. What happened?   1. What was the matter?

2. Did you break a bone?   2. How did you feel?

3. How did it happen?   3. Did you take any medicine?

4. Who were you with?   4. Did you call or go to the doctor?

5. What did you do?   5. Did you stay home? How long?

6. Did you go to the hospital?   6. Who took care of you?

7. How long did it take to get better? 7. How long did it take to feel better?

_____

_____

_____

_____

_____

_____

_____

_____

_____

Final Activity

I   **Create a story.** Read the questions and write short answers, making up a story as you go along. Then write the story in a paragraph below. Be creative! Add as many interesting details as you can. When you finish, share your story with your classmates. Everyone will have a different story.

1. Mr. Gonzalez was driving his car to school. He was very worried. What was he worried about? Why?_____

2. The weather was bad. Was it snowy or rainy?_____

3. He waited for the light. It turned green and he started to go. Suddenly, something came in front of him. What was it? _____

4. He didn't see it, and they had an accident. Was he badly injured or just hurt?

5. What did he hurt? _____

6. Did he get out of the car or stay in it? _____

7. How long did he wait for the police to arrive?_____

8. Did he go to the hospital or did he go to school? _____

9. Did he forget about his other problems, or did he continue to worry about them?

_____

_____
_____
_____
_____
_____
_____
_____
_____
_____
_____
_____

© Heinle & Heinle Publishers. All rights reserved.

What a Day!

Expressing admiration and disappointment *(text, page 151)*

A **Complete the conversations.** Use *What a/an . . .* to finish the conversations. You can also use some of these adjectives: *beautiful, delicious, great, fantastic, wonderful, interesting, busy, terrible, awful, boring.*

> **Example**
>
> (singer)
> A: Who's your favorite singer?
> B: Gloria Estefan.
> A: Yeah. *What a great singer!*

1. (accident)

   A: Did you read about that accident on Main Street? A bus hit a car. They took five people to the hospital.

   B: _____

2. (job)

   A: My aunt is a TV reporter. She interviews all different kinds of people. Then she reports on TV.

   B: _____

3. (week)

   A: I'm so happy it's Friday! I had so much work this week! I went to bed at 12:00 every night! And yesterday I had a soccer game.

   B: _____

4. (weather)

   A: How was your vacation?

   B: It was OK. But it rained, and it was cold and windy every day.

   A: _____

5. (color)

   A: Look at my new coat!

   B: _____ Where did you buy it?

6. (party)

   A: How was Mario's party?

   B: Not so great. I didn't know any people there. They didn't have any good music, so people didn't dance. I just sat on the couch and ate potato chips.

   A: _____

7. (cake)

   A: Try some of this cake. I made it last night.

   B: Thanks. Oh, this is great! _____

Name _____ Date _____

Time expressions with *the . . . before . . .* (text, page 152)

B **Questions with time expressions.** Answer the questions with complete sentences, using *the . . . before.*

> **Example**
>
> What was the day before yesterday? *The day before yesterday was Tuesday.*

1. What was the day before yesterday?

   _____

2. What did you do the day before yesterday?

   _____

3. Where did you go the week before last?

   _____

4. What did you do the night before last?

   _____

5. What was the month before last?

   _____

6. How old were you the year before last?

   _____

Both with nouns *(text, page 153)*
Both with pronouns *(text, page 154)*

C **Two neighbors.** Read about the two neighbors. Underline what they have in common. Then write two sentences about each thing they have in common. In the first sentence, use their names. In the second sentence, use pronouns.

Alicia Ramos is 16 and she lives on South Street. She goes to Winfield High School. She's tall and thin, and wears glasses. She gets up early in the morning, and takes her dog for a walk. In the afternoons, she visits friends or watches TV. She loves romantic movies. On weekends, she goes out with her boyfriend. She likes to eat Chinese food. Sometimes she cooks dinner for her boyfriend and her family. She's a great cook. She can cook wonderful desserts.

Margaret Wilson is 75 years old. She lives on South Street with her dog, Clyde. She's short and thin, and wears glasses. She gets up early every morning and takes Clyde for a walk. She usually visits friends in the morning and helps at the hospital in the afternoon. In the evening, she often watches TV. She loves romantic movies. On weekends, she goes out with her boyfriend. They like to go to the Chinese restaurant in Winfield. Margaret is a great cook, but she doesn't cook often. She can cook wonderful desserts.

> **Example**
>
> *Both Alicia and Margaret live on South Street.*
> *They both live on South Street.*

© Heinle & Heinle Publishers. All rights reserved.

1. _____

   _____

2. _____

   _____

3. _____

   _____

4. _____

   _____

5. _____

   _____

6. _____

   _____

7. _____

   _____

8. _____

   _____

Describing a person's personality *(text, page 156)*

D **People you know.** Write about people who you know, describing their personalities. Give positive and negative personality traits. Use some of the vocabulary below. Give examples of what people do to show their personality.

Vocabulary: hardworking / lazy / considerate / inconsiderate / reasonable / unreasonable / unforgiving / forgiving / unselfish / selfish / funny / patient / impatient / caring

> **Example**
>
> *My mother is very hardworking. She works all week and also takes care of four children. She is . . .*

1. _____

   _____

   _____

   _____

Name _____   Date _____

2. _____

   _____

   _____

   _____

3. _____

   _____

   _____

   _____

Making comparisons *(text, page 157)*

E **Compare.** Using the cues, write a sentence comparing the two things. Write your
own comparisons for the last two.

Example
fast: trains, cars
Trains are faster than cars.

1. warm: Greece, Germany   _____

2. cold: Moscow, Paris   _____

3. deep: Pacific Ocean, Mediterranean Sea   _____

4. hard: steel, gold   _____

5. nice: summer, winter   _____

6. long: December, February   _____

7. small: Japan, China   _____

8. old: Mexico City, New York City   _____

9. slow: buses, trains   _____

10. fast: computer, typewriter   _____

11. long: _____   _____

12. tall: _____   _____

© Heinle & Heinle Publishers. All rights reserved.

F **Your turn.** Using the cues, compare two people or things.

> **Example**
>
> Compare two people. (old)   _Thomas is older than Laura._

Compare two . . .

1. places (warm) _____

2. cities (cold)_____

3. rivers (long) _____

4. countries (small)_____

5. months (nice) _____

6. people (work hard) _____

7. people's hair (long) _____

8. people (tall) _____

9. buildings (old)_____

10. languages (hard) _____

11. people (run slow) _____

12. people (talk fast) _____

Irregular comparative forms: *good* and *bad*   (text, page 159)

G **What do you think?** Compare things and people, using *better than* or *worse than*.

> **Example**
>
> Compare two stores.   _Wilson's Department Store is better than Thompson's._

Compare two . . .

1. stores _____

2. good restaurants _____

3. bad restaurants _____

4. movies_____

5. seasons _____

6. TV programs _____

7. health problems _____

8. sports teams _____

9. musicians _____

10. newspapers_____

Name _____   Date _____

Final Activity

H **Country comparison.** Work together with a partner or in a small group. Choose two countries to compare. Pick countries that have some things in common. Write at least eight sentences, saying what they have in common and what is different. Then share your sentences with the class. In the vocabulary list are some possible words to use.

Vocabulary: . . . both . . . are / have / are famous for / grow / import / export / grow larger / smaller / older / nicer / warmer / colder / cooler / higher / faster / better than / worse than

Example

Countries: *England and the United States*
Both England and the United States have many
    famous actors and actresses.
They both have many historical buildings.
England is smaller than the United States.
The mountains in the United States are higher
    than the mountains in England.
The trains in England are better than the
    trains in the United States.

Countries: _____

_____

_____

_____

_____

_____

_____

_____

_____

_____

_____

_____

_____

_____

_____

_____

_____

_____

© Heinle & Heinle Publishers. All rights reserved.

How Are You Feeling?

Contrast between *come* and *go* *(text, page 163)*

A *Go* or *come*? Complete the sentences with the correct tense and form of *go* or *come*.

1. Yesterday Alicia _____ to the library to study for her test.
2. I invited Pierre to _____ to my house for dinner.
3. "Let's _____ to Marsha's house and listen to music."
4. My grandparents _____ to my house for dinner last night.
5. They usually _____ to visit us once a week. Sometimes they _____ to my aunt and uncle's house.
6. ALAN: Why don't you _____ with us to the movies?
   BOB: Sounds great, but I have to _____ home. I have to be there for dinner at 7:00.
7. Bob wanted to _____ with them to the movies, but he had to _____ home instead.
8. "I hope you _____ to see me again soon. I like to have visitors."
9. Silvia _____ to the city last weekend to visit her cousin.
10. "Why don't we _____ to the cafeteria to get a soda?"

If clauses in present tense *(text, pages 164-165)*

B "What if . . .?" Answer the questions, using complete sentences.

Example
What do you do if you have a bad earache? *If I have a bad earache, I call the doctor.*

1. What do you do if you have a headache?

   _____

2. What do you do if you have free time in the evening?

   _____

3. What do you do if you have extra money?

   _____

4. What do you say if you are late to class?

   _____

5. What do you do if you are nervous about something?

   _____

6. What do you drink if you are very thirsty?

   _____

7. What do you wear if the weather is very cold?

   _____

© Heinle & Heinle Publishers. All rights reserved.

Name _____   Date _____

Talking about a continuing condition *(text, page 166)*

C **Scrambled sentences.** Below is a conversation between two friends, Don and Ana. Unscramble each sentence of the conversation and write the words in the correct order.

Don and Ana see each other in a supermarket.
They last saw each other three years ago.
DON: Is that you, Ana?
ANA: Why hello, Don. What a surprise! How are you?
DON: Fine. What's new with you?
ANA: Not much, really.

DON: _____
(North Street / live / you / do / on / still / ?)

ANA: _____
(same / still / Yes / apartment / I / in / live / the / .)

DON: _____
(dog / And / you / big / have / still / do / that / ?)

ANA: _____
(have / Yes / Pepe / still / I / .)

DON: _____
(community college / at / you / Are / studying / the / still / ?)

ANA: _____
(finished / last / the / I / year / No / before / .)

DON: _____
(job / So / you / a / new / do / have / ?)

ANA: _____
(looking / No / still / I'm .)   (find / still / perfect / I / the / can't / job / .)

_____
(you / And / ?)   (still / you / studying / Are / business / ?)

DON: Yes._____
(finish / May / I / this / .)

ANA: _____
(with / you / parents / home / Do / live / your / still / at / ?)

DON: Yeah. _____
(apartment / still / I / an / have / don't / .)

ANA: _____
(store / at / still / Are / department / the / working / you / ?)

DON: _____
(job / I / No, / new / have / a / .)   (still / But / pay / doesn't / much / it.)

ANA: That's life! Well, nice to see you.
DON: Good to see you, too. Take care! And tell Pepe I said hello.
ANA: OK! Good luck with your school work. Bye.

D **Your turn.** Imagine that you see a friend at the supermarket. You last saw your friend two years ago. Write a conversation between yourself and your friend. Use exercise C as a model. Use as many lines as you need.

YOU: _____

_____

(FRIEND)

YOU: _____

_____

YOU: _____

_____

YOU: _____

_____

YOU: _____

_____

YOU: _____

_____

YOU: _____

_____

YOU: _____

_____

YOU: _____

_____

Name _____   Date _____

And so + be or modal auxiliaries *(text, page 168)*

E **Sentence completion.** Finish the sentences with *I* or with the name of someone you know. The sentences should be true.

> **Example**
>
> Sally is a good cook, *and so am I.*
> Sally is a good cook, *and so is my brother.*

1. Minh is tired, _____ .

2. Mohamed is studying English, _____ .

3. Martha should sleep more, _____ .

4. Tim should exercise more, _____ .

5. Kim can speak English well, _____ .

6. Jean can drive a car, _____ .

7. The Dominican Republic is a small country, _____ .

8. Brazil is a big country, _____ .

9. December is a cold month, _____ .

10. Gold is an expensive metal, _____ .

And so + do/does/did   *(text, page 169)*

F **George and Alice.** George and Alice are husband and wife. They are both 70 years old. They do everything the same. They also have two cats who often do what George and Alice do. Complete the sentences.

> **Example**
>
> Alice slept well last night, *and so did George.*

1. George sleeps well every night, _____ .

2. George got up at 6:30 this morning, _____ .

3. Alice always eats cereal for breakfast, _____ .

4. They drink milk with breakfast, _____ their cats.

5. Yesterday, George took a walk, _____ .

6. George and Alice like to take walks, _____ their cats.

7. Alice likes to watch the news on TV, _____ .

8. George reads after dinner, _____ .

9. Last week he finished a very long book, _____ .

10. George loves Alice, _____ their cats.

© Heinle & Heinle Publishers. All rights reserved.

G **Questionnaire.** Complete the questions below with ideas of your own. Then use the questionnaire to ask your classmates the questions. Find two people to answer *yes* to each question. Write names on the questionnaire.

Example
Do you *like to eat Chinese food*?　*Marie*　*Tomas*   Can you *drive a car*?　　　　　　*Pierre*　*Ana*

1. Do you _____ ? _____ _____
2. Do you _____ ? _____ _____
3. Can you _____ ? _____ _____
4. Can you _____ ? _____ _____
5. Should you _____ ? _____ _____
6. Are you _____ ? _____ _____
7. Are you _____ ? _____ _____
8. Did you _____ ? _____ _____
9. Did you _____ ? _____ _____
10. Did you _____ ? _____ _____

H **Report.** Write sentences for each question, reporting what you found out.

Example
Marie likes to eat Chinese food, and so does Tomas.   *Pierre can drive a car, and so can Ana.*

1. _____
2. _____
3. _____
4. _____
5. _____
6. _____
7. _____
8. _____
9. _____
10. _____